Theda 1

Theda Bara

A Biography of the Silent Screen Vamp, with a Filmography

RONALD GENINI

McFarland & Company, Inc., Publishers
Jefferson, North Carolina, and London

1996

For my wife

Frontispiece: Theda Bara as *Cleopatra* (1917); courtesy
Academy of Motion Picture Arts and Sciences.

The present work is a reprint of the library bound edition of
Theda Bara: A Biography of the Silent Screen Vamp,
with a Filmography, *first published in 1996 by McFarland.*

LIBRARY OF CONGRESS CATALOGUING-IN-PUBLICATION DATA

Genini, Ronald
    Theda Bara : a biography of the silent screen vamp, with a
filmography / by Ronald Genini.
        p.   cm.
    Includes bibliographical references and index.

    ISBN 978-0-7864-6918-5
    softcover : acid free paper ∞

    1. Bara, Theda, 1890[sic]–1955.   2. Motion picture actors
and actresses — United States — Biography.   I. Title.
PN2287.B178G46   2012
791.43'028'092 — dc20   [B]   96-11764

BRITISH LIBRARY CATALOGUING DATA ARE AVAILABLE

Front cover image: Theda Bara as Cleopatra in *Cleopatra*, 1917 (Photofest);
border © 2012 Shutterstock

Manufactured in the United States of America

*McFarland & Company, Inc., Publishers
    Box 611, Jefferson, North Carolina 28640
        www.mcfarlandpub.com*

Contents

Preface

I heard of Theda Bara occasionally while growing up. I probably even saw the newspaper on the day she died, but it did not really register with me, as I was only eight. My grandmother may have mentioned her, as she always mentioned the actors and actresses she recognized on television's afternoon movies — especially the dead ones. Occasional references to her in various histories, novels and films undoubtedly helped to spark the interest which developed into this book.

I began to wonder who this character was, this vampire lady, this first star who is now nearly forgotten. For let there be no misunderstanding: Theda Bara, with her talents and her foibles, was America's first star — a totally created character, one who was in real life no more like the creature created by a film studio than an apple is like a grape. She was given an invented name, an evil persona, and a fictional history, and the public swallowed it; meanwhile others, less virtuous, were upheld as the epitome of innocence. The public believed. Why? Mencken said that one could not go broke underestimating the intelligence of the American public, and this case would seem to support his contention.

I do not want to overstate Theda Bara's importance. Compared to such early giants of the film industry as D. W. Griffith, Charlie Chaplin, and the super-producers Fox, DeMille, Zukor and Laemmle, she is a relatively minor figure. Consequently, little can be found concerning her career other than a few words in the larger film history studies. Yet her career as screen vamp should not be underrated, for it is she who began the long line of Hollywood stars who, with little real acting ability of their own, have been built up by publicity departments into super-personalities who fade quickly when public interest can no longer be sustained on publicity alone. She was the first sex goddess, exploited until there was no new titillation left to give the public, unable to fall back on native talent. A long line follows her, with most of her successors meeting a similar sad end thanks to the fickleness of the public.

There is little difference between the sort of publicity Theda Bara received and that accorded Marilyn Monroe, for once Hollywood learned that the public would accept what it was told — for a while at least — and that deceptive publicity could contribute to enormous profits, the process would be repeated innumerable times. And Theda Bara's created personality — puffed by impossible honors, glinting through tons of makeup, flirting into a camera not permitted to remain fixed on her for too long — reaped huge profits as Fox showed Hollywood a path from which it has never turned. Except for the films of Mary Pickford and Charlie Chaplin, Theda Bara's films returned more money per dollar of investment than those of any other star of her time.

Her films were trite, often poorly acted, extravagant and crude. That meant little, for the public packed the cinema houses and even rioted over her. She meanwhile fancied herself the public's star, without malice or fraud, and, for a while at least, they were faithful to their Vampire Queen.

I came to feel sorrow for La Bara — not pity, but sorrow that she had been so neglected, having never been the subject of a real biography. I decided to fill that gap. I have enjoyed uncovering the facts of her life and weaving them together in this biography as I have enjoyed few other intellectual tasks.

But it has not been a task that I performed alone. There are many to thank, and if any are missed, it is through innocent omission and not by intent.

First and foremost, my thanks go to Kathy Barberich, a writer for the *Fresno Bee*, who assisted me with many hours of editorial comment. Without her unselfish help the refined work you hold would not have been. By a happy coincidence, her mother is named Theda because her grandmother thought it was a fine name for a girl.

I would also like to thank Gayla King Jamison (formerly Gayla Hamilton) who allowed me to use information she had independently uncovered for a master's thesis on Theda Bara in 1972.

There have been other unselfish people behind this work. The principal of Theda's high school, David A. Shepherd, sent me a copy of her graduate yearbook and a copy of a story she had written for her school newspaper. The late Cantor Michael Loring of Fresno's Temple Beth Israel assisted with information on the culture of the Jewish immigrants from Russian Poland. Another was Hyman Belzberg, who took time out from a busy schedule to show my wife and me around Theda's old home in Beverly Hills. He was quite surprised by our visit, yet displayed the greatest hospitality and interest in the project.

Still others were Diane Kisro of Venice, California, who was a nurse at the retirement home where Theda's sister, Lori, spent her last years; Dr. Edward Furstman of West Los Angeles, who was Theda and Charles Brabin's dentist; Professor Robert Slayton of Chapman College; and Bob Coleman, the owner of the Hollywood Poster Exchange. On August 29, 1990, these kind people gave of their time, showing Theda memorabilia.

Not to be forgotten is the late June Millarde Stanley of Gaithersburg, Maryland, Theda's goddaughter. Ms. Stanley was able to fill me in on various aspects of Theda's personality as perceived by a young girl who was very close to her.

Others to thank include the staffs of the California Historical Society and the Sutro Library in San Francisco; the State Library in Sacramento; the History Center in Los Angeles; the librarians of UCLA's Film Collection Special Section (especially Brigitte Kueppers); the librarians of the Academy of Motion Picture Arts and Sciences in Beverly Hills (especially Sam Gill, Robert Cushman and Allison Pindler); the Museum of Modern Art Film Study Center in New York City; the archivists of the University of Cincinnati; the librarians of the Cincinnati Historical Society; the genealogy librarians of the Church of Jesus Christ of Latter-Day Saints in Fresno; the staff of Forest Lawn Cemetery in Glendale; Leonard Panaggio of Rhode Island, Alison C. Gagnon of Arizona, and Lynne W. Alkire of Illinois for their constant encouragement; the residents of the Motion Picture Retirement Home who shared their memories; and those who took the time and trouble to answer my ads in the *Los Angeles Times*, the *Hollywood Reporter*, and *The Californians*. Among the latter I especially thank Bryan Plank of LaJolla, Mrs. E. Schieffelin of Los Angeles, Jay Hicks of Chula Vista, Virginia McClintock of West Covina, and Virginia Leach of Piedmont, all in California, and to Beverly Stout of Mississippi who suggested the re-publication of this book in a paperback format.

I also wish to thank the staff of *The Californians* for publishing my article on Theda in July 1994.

In conclusion, I would like to thank my three sons, Thomas (and his wife Arianna), Justin and Nicholas for their patience with their dad during the three years I labored on this task, and their mother, my wife Roberta. If it were not for her help and encouragement, I could never have completed this project. It is to her that I lovingly dedicate this book.

ONE.
A Nice Jewish Girl from Cincinnati

*E*ven today, decades after her death, the name of Theda Bara conjures images of mystery, eroticism, power, beauty, intrigue. The name, she herself said, had emotional value "in a world in which romance is a food all hearts crave." Who (or what) was she? "Always I have been a Charlatan, a register of human emotions.... What difference does it make where I was born? ... For years my emotional display has been accredited to my Arab blood.... Who knows, who cares, but I myself?" she wrote for an article in 1919. "I'm really a nice Jewish girl [from Cincinnati]. And that's all."

Or was it? Theda Bara may have described herself better than any biographer with one word in 1919. Was she a charlatan? Did she represent herself as someone she was not?

In the Columbarium of Memory in Glendale, California's Forest Lawn Cemetery, in the same kingdom of the dead wherein reside the likes of W. C. Fields (1879–1946) and Liberace (1919–1987), is a very plain plaque behind which lie the ashes of Theda Bara Brabin, née Theodosia Goodman. Situated at eye level, its plainness belies its contents. What casual observer would know its significance?

She was not only the first real star but also the first victim of the star system. She was a feminist (and sex symbol) ahead of her time. Did she know what she was doing when she signed the contract which propelled her to stardom, and does what happened to her still happen in Hollywood? She was famous for her beauty and her work broke ground in women's history as well as cinematic history. Her crypt's simple message, "Theda Bara Brabin 1955," tells nothing of the lovable, talented, enjoyable person, a flamboyant performer frustrated by mediocrity, nor does it give the least clue to her significance.

What made her? Why did she achieve — and fall from — the pinnacle of popularity in so short a time, and was there life after acting?

Theodosia Goodman was born in Cincinnati on July 20, supposedly in 1890. (Subsequent events in her life would indicate that the actual date was 1885, though many encyclopedias and biographical dictionaries still report 1890 as her birthdate.) She was the second of three, having a brother named Marque and a sister named Lori. She was called Theodosia after the beautiful but tragic only daughter of Aaron Burr, the vice president who served under Jefferson, killed Alexander Hamilton in a duel and was tried for treason for his attempted invasion of Mexico and his intent to sever the Ohio Valley from the Union. Theodosia Burr Alston's life had romantic appeal in the nineteenth century. She comforted her father during his treason trial, took charge of his affairs when he went abroad into exile, lost her infant son to fever and, at age 30, was lost at sea while sailing to see her father.

Prior to 1908 Ohio law did not require compulsory birth registration, but a Cincinnati man born in 1885 said that she was in the first and second grades with him in an Avondale school in 1891-92 (though very intelligent, she was hardly such a prodigy as to be in elementary school at the age of one). There is a manuscript in the New York Public Library Theater Collection written by a high school classmate who said that she was with "Theo" at the University of Cincinnati in 1904. In the early 1960s, when Wallace Davies of the University of Pennsylvania was researching several silent film stars, he met an old classmate of Theodosia's. When he mentioned the 1890 birthdate, she hooted with laughter, but would not reveal her own age or exactly when she had been in school. In the first week of July 1900 the census taker recorded that she was 14 (and that her mother was 39). She graduated from high school in 1903.

It was not unlikely that as an actress Theda would "under-exaggerate" her age, for, like Louella Parsons, she believed that a woman who would not keep her true age a secret would preserve nothing else. Her sister's birth certificate places the arrival of Lori (originally called Estie, then Loro) in October 1897; some sources give Marque's original name as Paul, but that same census taker listed 12-year-old Marque as Mark.

Before the great migration of Jews to America from Russian Poland to escape Alexander III's pogroms in the 1880s, there were a few who began in the 1870s to sense discrimination. Among these was a tailor who, in the confusion of immigration inspection, received the last name of Goodman. He hailed from a tiny hamlet called Chorzele in the province of Ostrołęka, about 75 miles (120 kilometers) north of Warsaw and then just shy of the German border (today, deep in Poland, it boasts a service station). Bernard Goodman eventually found his way west to Cincinnati, Ohio, where he settled down to his tailoring trade with some success and married Pauline Louise Françoise de Coppet, an intelligent, well-bred French-Swiss woman born of a French father and German mother in the watchmaking Swiss city of La Chaux de Fonds, canton of Neuchâtel, in what she claimed was 1869. In 1871 Goodman, who gave his age as 18, became an American citizen. Pauline was born in 1861, came to America in 1868 and married in 1882.

Goodman, Theda's father, was described variously as a tailor and as a small manufacturer, so it seems not unlikely that he was a small-scale clothing manufacturer. He was listed in Cincinnati directories from 1881 until 1905, and from 1899 to 1904 was listed with the wholesale clothing firm of Ochs, Weil and Goodman.

Pauline Goodman, the daughter of François Barranger de Coppet, was listed as a seller of hair goods in Cincinnati's Emory Arcade from 1878 to 1881 under her maiden name and, in 1885-86, under her married name. In both instances she was in partnership with another lady, first a Mrs. Rena Dunkelmeyer and then a Frieda Deeg. Like her to-be-famous daughter, it seems obvious that she shaved a few years off her real age over the years.

Infant Theodosia, showing no sign of the blonde hair she spoke of having (courtesy UCLA Arts Library, Special Collections).

As a young girl Theda, known as "Theo" to her family, was blonde, but nightly she prayed that she would grow up tall with black hair and that she would become an actress. While she only reached five feet six inches (158.4 centimeters), dye took care of the hair and she did become one of the tribe of Thespis.

While it boasted no Broadway, Cincinnati was a fertile ground for a young woman who wanted to make a career in the entertainment field. The city, the nation's eighth largest in population in 1900, was unquestionably an important railroad hub and manufacturing center, and was the cultural center for the entire Ohio Valley as well. Since the 1870s, the city's proudest ornament was the Music Hall and Exposition Building, an edifice of cornices and spires, columned doorways, arched windows and fretted rooflines.

The Music Hall held 4,600 people and accommodated 120 orchestra members and 1,000 singers as well as the world's largest organ (6,237 pipes). Its erection was followed by the Cincinnati College of Music. Along with meat packing, brewing and the printing of McGuffey Readers, Cincinnati swelled with music.

Before Theo started school the family moved to 823 Hutchins Avenue in Avondale. Avondale was a new district in Cincinnati, largely Jewish, with nice middle-class homes. There they rented a home and had two white American female servants, Ida Seyberth and Anna Tunnig, both a little older than Theo. Theo's rabbi, Louis Grossman, later a fan of the film star, remembered Theo as a member of one of his confirmation classes.

In addition to praying for a change in her physical appearance, she started on her way to an acting career by giving verse recitations and dramatic readings at public functions. These included such literary gems as "The Dirty Faced Brat" and "Which Shall It Be?" According to one story, her rendition of the latter caused the school principal to remove his glasses in order to wipe away his tears (presumably of tenderness).

Writing about herself in 1919, Theda recalled her beginnings as an actress:

> I always had the instincts of an actress. The difficulty sometimes in my childhood ambition was to get an audience. I needed advertising, no one knew what an actress I was. So one day brother, in a splendid impulse of gratitude to me for having rescued him from some boy scrape, promoted my first public appearance. With the practical but skeptical outlook of the masculine nature, my brother agreed to give me a test. He arranged the performance for me in the barn of "Old Man Dyker."
>
> Old man Dyker's theater was not within the fire laws, but the ventilation was almost as good as the average motion-picture theater. It was also about as decorative. The price of admission was five pins, but that would not have been enough to attract so large an audience, even with the talent announced. So Buddie, my brother, realized that there should be some other interest than merely a star performer to draw the crowd.
>
> So, it was announced that at the end of the performance, the entire audience would be served with lemonade and cookies. Those cookies were famous in the neighborhood, they were made by the cooking star of the country, "Our Lily." Lily was a Swede, beautiful and efficient, a sort of domestic vampire who went wrong subsequently.
>
> When the audience was collected in the barn, Buddie, with his sleeves rolled up, was prepared to deal summarily with any offender who dared to leave before the performance was over. Furthermore he was ticket-collector, the most determined manager I ever had.
>
> I gave the entire entertainment alone. I sang, I danced, I recited, and how happy I was to make this exhibition for myself. No star has ever enjoyed such absolute dominion as I had that day. It was the dawn of my career.
>
> Even then I knew that hundreds of thousands of people would some day come to see me as an actress. Of course, the audiences that came afterward have been more sophisticated. My first audience was tempted by the pitcher of lemonade that stood conspicuously where they could see it as they came in. The temptation of the audiences that have come to see me since, may not have been so mild. Buddie will never admit that the lemonade had anything

Theodosia as a child in two poses taken as a set (courtesy UCLA Arts Library, Special Collections).

to do with the success of my first public appearance. He insists that only the terrific sight of the bared arms of this angry pugilist of seven years, guarding the door, made my success certain. He still claims his part of the success of that event.

Walnut Hills High School is Cincinnati's college prep school and since its founding, it has required an admission test. Theo entered Walnut Hills as a member of the class of 1903, and while there are no existing records of her coursework, she must have made an impression as a member of the Dramatic Club and as a literary staff member of *The Gleam*, the school paper. In 1902, when a senior, she wrote a highly literate short story about a couple of happy marriages resulting from a Christmas party. In none of the four photographs depicting her in her graduating yearbook does one see a hint of the allure which would later look out from the silver screen.

In the senior class play in May 1903 she played the minor role of Mrs. Mountchessington in Tom Taylor's *Our American Cousin* (the same play Abraham Lincoln happened to have been attending when he was assassinated).

Of her an admiring schoolmate wrote, "Theo excels in the literary art, and her work bears the stamp of true genius. Her literary ability, however, is not the only claim she has to fame — her histrionic talent is a characteristic well known to those who have witnessed a performance of the Senior Dramatic Club. She is an entertaining conversationalist."

For the quotation which would symbolize her life and goals, she chose, "With heart and fancy all on fire, To climb the hill of fame."

Following her graduation from high school she attended the University of Cincinnati for two years, and was thus one of the few early female movie stars (if not the only one) to have a college background. During that time she began to take note of a new phenomenon: the movies. It was at the town's only movie theater that Theo fell in love with the big screen. Following her death, the *Cincinnati Enquirer*'s editor wrote an editorial of his memory of the young woman in the Avon Theater: "[In] the old Avon movie theater on Rockdale Avenue when the lights went on after the show we could not help but noticing a striking-looking young woman sitting quietly by herself in one of the rear rows. She always seemed to be there and stayed through all the performances. We were told that she wanted to be a movie actress."

In 1905, when Theo was 20, the family may have moved to New York City, perhaps to foster her theatrical ambitions, and she may have attended dramatic school there. The father's Cincinnati business was not listed in that year's directory, and the family was not listed in the city directories after that year.

TWO.

Dyed Hair, Painted Faces and Hollywood

*F*or the next few years Theodosia Goodman's career was minor and poorly documented. She may have been in an obscure open-air Shakespearean troupe which played the English countryside, but despite her claims (upheld by no less than *Variety*), she appeared in no Parisian Theatre Antoine. Dyeing her hair and painting her face to become "truly dramatic," she slunk onstage in bizarre and exotic dresses.

Taking her mother's maiden name as her stage name at age 23, Theodosia De Coppet made her debut on Broadway and was cast in the Henry Savage production of Ferenc Molnar's *The Devil*, playing (in her words) "only a small part" as Mme. Schleswig. With Edwin Stevens in the title role, it opened at the Garden Theatre on Broadway on August 18, 1908. Since this play was not copyrighted in the United States, a competing version starring George Arliss opened the same night. On Broadway the rival production had outplayed Theo's by about 70 performances when, in November, Savage decided to take the play on tour. Stevens was replaced by Henry Dixey, who had played the role in Chicago.

In 1910, by the time she was 25, Theo was playing second parts at a Yiddish theater on the Lower East Side. But the following year, in 1911, she landed a part in the touring company of the popular musical *The Quaker Girl*, with DeWolf Hopper (1858–1935) in the lead. His later-famous wife, Hedda Hopper (1890–1966), was also in the cast and recalled that "Theodosia played a Frenchwoman with an accent that wouldn't fool a five-year-old. Oh, brother!"

By this time Theo was known in theatrical circles as a very ambitious actress adept in *femme fatale* roles, who dabbled in spiritualism. This, more than her spurious French accent, intrigued Hopper. Theda later avowed that her spirit contact advised her to try her luck in "the shadow world," as the movies were then known in certain circles. At first she had little luck.

When, in 1914 at the age of 29, Theo realized her career was not progressing,

7

she began to haunt the movie studios in nearby New Jersey. One of the studio heads she met was Cecil B. DeMille (1881-1959), who later said he could have kicked himself for "failing to take much notice of Theodosia Goodman although she used to come to our office hopefully when she heard that we might be casting."

Even though she later claimed that she started as a star, the fact remains that she had her share of bit parts. "I started out as a star," she liked to say, "and remained a star." Whether she did is debatable. Director Frank Powell made her only a nameless "face in the crowd" in *The Stain* rather than bill her as an extra so that the name would be new when used to introduce her as a leading lady.

Recalling her early film attempts, she told movie historian Alan Brock in the 1950s that after *The Devil,*

> I was given my first role in a motion picture—*The Stain* at Fort Lee, N.J. Did you know that most of the motion pictures at that time were filmed at Fort Lee [Bergen County], New Jersey? — It was really the Hollywood of its day. Many of the performers in New York stage plays worked there even when they were acting in a play at night. That is — except the truly eminent stage names. They came later.
>
> Gradually one role after another led me to Portland, Oregon, where I was signed to do a complete season of stock. You know — September to June — and a new role each week. That was excellent training for a newcomer, I assure you.
>
> After that season was over, it was only a short jump to Los Angeles.... The movies — well — somehow I suppose it was inevitable. Though I always preferred the stage. I love the perfect speech, and grand manner. I never truly intended to remain in motion pictures so long ... but c'est la vie....

At the time Theo's film debut in *The Stain* was produced in New Jersey, Hollywood was but a sleepy little town where the exciting news, the really big news, of each day was the arrival of the stagecoach, and later the interurban train from Los Angeles. Starting as the 120-acre Wilcox Ranch in 1887, it was granted a post office in 1897 and was incorporated in 1903 with a population of 700. In 1910 the voters, realizing that its arid location resulted in an inadequate water supply, chose annexation to Los Angeles.

Hollywood became the refuge for the Eastern moviemakers who were escaping the monopoly of Thomas Edison's Motion Picture Patent Company. In 1894 Edison had invented the Kinetoscope, the original motion picture projector. Within a few years he made many patented improvements and created the monopolistic Patents Company. All theaters were classified and assessed a weekly license fee and restricted to the use of film and projection equipment manufactured by members of the Patent Company.

In 1907 a Chicago moviemaker "Colonel" William Selig (1864-1948), impressed by Los Angeles Chamber of Commerce hyperbole concerning sunshine and ideal outdoor moviemaking conditions, moved west and started on Olive Street. He was soon followed by others fleeing from Eastern monopolies dominated by Edison's company — D. W. Griffith's Biograph Company on 12th Street, the New York Motion Picture Company, the Kalem, the I.M.P., the Rex, the Power and the Bison companies in 1909 alone. In 1910 David Horsley's Nestor Company moved from Brooklyn to a studio at Sunset and Gower streets and produced Hollywood's first picture, *Her Indian Hero*. The year 1911 saw the arrival of 15 companies; 1912 brought the Famous Players–Lasky Film Company, the Vitagraph Company and Sennet Studio. In 1913 Hollywood had grown to 7800 people, most of whom were connected to the movie industry. Property values skyrocketed, with lemon groves once bought for $700 per acre now fetching $10,000 per acre as subdivision properties.

In December 1915 William Fox of the Fox Film Corporation sent some of his actors west from New York on a fact-finding trip. They were impressed by what they saw and bought the Selig Studio property at 1845 Allessandro Street. The following July Fox started filming comedies at that location. Five additional comedy companies sprang up, and the Fox Company kept pace with the growth.

Soon Fox realized that the three-quarter-acre studio could not accommodate his growing company. In late 1916, Fox purchased the former Thomas Dixon Studio, 5 1/2 acres, on the west side of Western Avenue at Sunset Boulevard.

The Fox Film Corporation had its origins in 1913, when as the Box Office Attractions and Film Rental Company it filmed *Life's Shop Window* on Staten Island at a cost of $6,000. Fox was born in the tiny Hungarian village of Tolcsva (or Tulchva), some 125 miles or 200 kilometers northeast of Budapest in 1879 of Jewish parents who changed their name from Fried to Fox when they immigrated to America the following year. Beset by poverty in the Lower East Side, Fox tried to rise above it in the 1890s by teaming up with comedian Craig Gordon in a vaudeville act which never quite succeeded. The failed vaudevillian went into the rag-cleaning business and managed to save $1,000; thus many of the directors and actors he later employed referred to him with some contempt as "a pants presser."

In 1904 he was hoodwinked into spending his life savings to buy his first theater in Brooklyn. The future movie mogul was sharp enough to turn the venture into a success and soon owned not one but 15 movie houses in the metropolis, forming the Greater New York Rental Company. Fearful of growing competition, Edison's organization tried to squeeze him out of the industry. Fox sued for $6 million and settled out of court for $300,000.

At first Fox purchased movies from the Balboa Company, but eventually he sent stage producer J. Gordon Edwards to Europe to study filmmaking as a prelude to producing his own. His story writer was his wife Eve, and with the moderate success of *Life's Shop Window*, he determined to go beyond Fort Lee into the big leagues. Sharp-eyed, beak-nosed and handicapped by a crippled arm, he was eventually able to challenge Universal and Famous Players–Lasky.

Fox attracted a large amount of investment capital, including the interest of important backers such as John Dryden, president of Newark's Prudential Insurance Company. This large capital base made it possible for Fox to pay generous salaries to rising new stars, budget his productions at above-average costs and promote them lavishly.

One of his actors, Jack Gilbert (1897-1936), not satisfied with the pants presser appellation, stated, "Fox doesn't have a friend in the world, because he's mean, cheap, vulgar and he's notorious for breaking his word. He's a fifth-grade dropout with an absolute contempt for education. Do you know what he said to me?" he asked his wife Leatrice. "He said, 'Why should I read a book when I can buy the bum who wrote it?'"

Twenty years later, in 1933, Fox told muckraker Upton Sinclair (1878–1968) that he sought to produce serious and moral movies, making it a company rule "that any clergyman may have any Fox film free of charge at any time for showing in any synagogue, church or Sunday school, any hospital, orphan asylum, or home for the aged."

That was before Fox went bankrupt and before he went to prison for obstructing justice in an investigation of his financial irregularities and for attempted jury tampering. The stock market crash eventually reduced his $300 million fortune to $18 million, and he filed for bankruptcy. In 1935 Fox Film Corporation merged with Twentieth Century Pictures to form a new company, Twentieth Century–Fox. For several years he was in and out of court in connection with complicated bankruptcy proceedings, and in 1941 he was sentenced to 366 days behind bars for conspiracy and defrauding the government. In 1944 he made an unsuccessful comeback attempt, and in 1948 he offered as a public service a documentary on Sister Elizabeth Kenny's polio treatments. He died in 1952, at age 73.

For all of Fox's filmmaking status in the early days, he was not an original pioneer. Nor were most of the other early producers. That honor goes to D. W. Griffith (1875–1948), a Kentuckian who played his first leading role when he was 32. Prior to Griffith's 1909 arrival in Southern California, production heads (usually businessmen, lawyers and engineers with little or no training in films) insisted that one- and two-reelers, at about ten minutes per reel, were all that the low intelligence of the moviegoers could comprehend. Nor, they insisted, would audiences appreciate close-up action shots, preferring instead (they surmised) the front-row-center position then afforded by stationary cameras. Underestimating the mentality of audiences and their willingness to pay for improved entertainment, the producers were naturally taken aback by the success enjoyed by Griffith's controversial *Birth of a Nation*. The movie sparked a revolution in filmmaking, and one of those who rode the wave of this revolution was Fox.

The time was right for Theo's entrance into the film world.

THREE.
Theodosia Becomes Theda; Woman Becomes Vampire

Seventeen years before Theodosia De Coppet became Theda, Philip Burne-Jones showed *The Vampire* at the 1897 summer exhibition in London's New Gallery. The painting was of a woman — pale, dark-eyed, magnetic, surreal — clad in white, on which played a ghastly green glow. At her feet was stretched out her male victim, bare-chested and bloodlessly pale. Intended as a shock picture, it was most often described as gruesome. Burne-Jones' cousin Rudyard Kipling (1865–1936) contributed a poem to the catalog of the New Gallery exhibit. Also called "The Vampire," it was six stanzas of misogyny which began

> A fool there was and he made his prayer
> (Even as you and I!)
> To a rag and a bone and a hank of hair
> (We call her the woman who did not care)
> But the fool he called her his lady fair -
> (Even as you and I!)

The poem, which was inspired by the painting, was widely circulated in the United States where Bram Stoker's *Dracula* appeared that same year. Together the novel, painting, and poem created a vogue for the female vampire, the worthless but irresistible creature who sucks the love and life out of a man.

Profiting from this vogue was Porter Emerson Browne, a hack who turned the poem into a play (1906) and a novel (1909), both called *A Fool There Was*. In 1909-10 at New York's Liberty Theatre the play was staged. It was a hit.

Browne turned the Fool of the poem into a Wall Street banker turned diplomat for his play. The Fool was recalled from England by the American president after he had disgraced himself by adultery with his lady fair. The ingredients were familiar to American melodrama audiences of the previous 60 years: drink, debt and marital infidelity. There was a difference, however, as noted by Alex Walker, historian of cinematic sexuality. In this play the focus was on the home-breaker, a sexually aggressive woman who took pleasure in her lover's destruction — i.e., the vampire.

This was a new type of vampire, a far cry from the earlier ones. Those had been supernatural creatures who lived on their victims' blood. The cruel fifteenth century Romanian prince, Vlad the Impaler, and the seventeenth century lesbian Hungarian Countess Elizabeth Bathory (who was brought to orgasm by the slaughter of hundreds of young girls), had been literature's prototypes of vampires, although the genre goes back to Aristophanes's Lamiae. The Lamiae were beautiful serpent women who used to seduce, enervate and suck the blood of travelers.

Their victims were drawn into their arms by an unholy sexual charm, as in Stoker's *Dracula.* The traveler, Harker, waits for the three women at Castle Dracula, passively longing for their white teeth and ruby lips (feeling "a wicked, burning desire that they would kiss him"). As to the other sex, how many women bitten by the male vampire swooned with pleasure at the penetration of *his* canines?

But the new vampire, created by Burne-Jones and Kipling and brought to life by Theda née Theodosia, was the "psychic vampire," in the words of Montague Summers, a student of vampires in Europe. She was a very human, non-supernatural creature. Sexual conquest was still a prime factor of her vampirism, but physical blood played no part in it. Figuratively blood did play a part — blood being life and she draining him of life — but not via her fangs. Her perverse motive was mere destruction.

The psychic vampire was usually female while the Dracula-type vampire was usually male. Summers and others who have analyzed the vampire also differentiate between the psychic vampire and the *femme fatale,* a literary product contemporary with the psychic vampire. The psychic vampire and the femme fatale both possess irresistible sexual magnetism, but there they part company. The femme fatale, unlike the psychic vampire, has no spooky quasi-supernatural exoticism. She is physical, not demonic; neurotic, not evil; and, unlike the vampire she possesses a conscience, albeit a suppressed one.

After his initial success Fox felt a strong need to offer an antidote to movie saccharine as typified by Blanche Sweet (1895–1986), Arlene Pretty, Louise Lovely, and "America's Sweetheart," fair-haired Mary Pickford. So he decided to project the vampire onto the silver screen. Sometime before 1914 he bought the screen rights from author Browne. Some years later Fox recounted to Upton Sinclair how he came to cast Theodosia De Coppet as the evil seductress in the film.

Fox said he consulted with Robert Hilliard (1857–1927), the play's Broadway producer and leading man, who told him how the actresses who played the vampire on the stage tended to let success go to their heads and had to be replaced.

"Put the girl you choose under contract," he advised Fox. "She will not make the part; the part will make her." This was extremely important advice. When Frank Powell, the film's Griffith-trained director, discovered an almost unknown actress, she was put under contract to Fox, not only to play the part but to be the part.

The actress was Theodosia De Coppet, who had been making the casting rounds to the many movie studios in New Jersey. When she applied at Powell's office he was im-

A vampish photo taken in 1915 by famed San Francisco photographer Arnold Genthe, who photographed nearly every great personage in the world between 1895 and his death in 1942 (courtesy UCLA Arts Library, Special Collections).

pressed by her potential and sent her on location to the Petit Trianon Theater, at Lake Ronkonkomo on Long Island. There she gained her first film experience as a face in the crowd of the Pathé film *The Stain*. Powell was further impressed by her ability to take direction.

Just as David Selznick (1902–1965) would milk the publicity potential in the 1939 hunt for someone to play Scarlet O'Hara, Powell hyped his consideration of several noted actresses for *Fool*'s lead, including Virginia Pearson (1886–1958), a star of *The Stain* and a veteran of the Broadway play in 1910, but after seeing Theodosia De Coppet at work he decided to offer her the vampire lead in Fox's new movie.

Powell conferred with Fox, who liked the rushes and thought Theodosia was a natural. He also couldn't afford a "real" star. Theodosia got the job.

This was a lucky break for Theo since her legitimate career was not really sending up skyrockets and she was not getting any younger. Still she was reluctant to play such a daring, unvirtuous role. In fact, as she stated in 1919, "up to [that time] I had not only no desire to turn my talents to [movies], but my mind was emphatically against it." Film historian DeWitt Bodeen doubts this claim. In any case, her precarious financial condition persuaded her to take the plunge. She claimed that when she decided to accept the role she also determined to apply herself diligently for five years, then retire and live on the loot. This sounds like an attempt to make sour grapes sweeter, in view of the fact that she was released by Fox after five short years.

To create this leading villainess, some alterations in Theo's "circumspect and demure" outward personality were essential. She was the first movie star around whom a real publicity campaign was built. She actually gave the campaign its first push. One day when Fox asked her where she was born she responded, "It wouldn't be exciting to say Cincinnati, would it? Suppose we say the Sahara Desert?"

"You don't need a press agent," was Fox's comment.

Interviewed years later by Upton Sinclair, Fox recalled,

> One day it was conceived in our publicity department that we had had every type of woman on the screen except an Arabian; our publicity director felt that the public would like an Arabian. He conceived the story that this Miss Goodman was born in Arabia — her father was an Arab and her mother a French woman who had played the theatres in Paris.
>
> So we took "Arab," spelling it backwards, made it "Bara," and shortened the first name "Theodosia" to "Theda" and thus the name "Theda Bara." Then the director said, "Now let's not settle on this until we see if it will go over. Let me invite the newspapers to an interview and see if they will swallow this."
>
> He dressed her in the regular Arabian costume, and surrounded her with the proper atmosphere, and then the newspaper boys all came in. He said, "I want you to meet Miss Bara," and gave them her history. He said she didn't speak a word of English. The newspaper men left that day and said that the Fox Film Corporation had discovered the greatest living actress in the world.

To the average American of the time an Arab was an exotic creature, perhaps familiar to stereopticon owners who had sets of pictures from the Holy Land. They were usually identified as Turks, since the Ottoman Empire owned most of the Arabian lands. Americans had little knowledge of Arabic-speaking people, having only occasional contact with Arab immigrants peddling rugs, sewing materials and leather goods.

To turn the created villainess into a star after the 1915 success of *A Fool There Was,* Selig and Goldfarb presented her to the press on a visit to Chicago. Major M. L. C. Funkhouser, Chicago's film censor, declined to meet her. Louella Parsons (1893–1972), then an aspiring Chicago journalist, recalled that Ms. Bara was driven in a "dead-white" limousine attended by two "Nubian" footmen to the press conference at the Blackstone Hotel.

> The day was hotter than the proverbial hinges of the proverbial hot spot. We dripped little beads of perspiration in anticipation as we waited in an anteroom in Theda's hotel suite at the Blackstone for the summons to the presence. Mr. Hollander (the "Daily News") had just voiced the opinion that it was so hot The Vamp had probably melted into her own eyelash goo when the press agent appeared in our midst and said: "Miss Bara will be a moment longer. She is not yet acclimated to this Northern weather!"
>
> No more were the words out of his mouth than the door of an adjoining room began to open noiselessly and seemingly without the aid of human hands — and there, exposed in unbelievable splendor, sat the Queen of Sirens, draped to the teeth in magnificent furs. "Miss Bara," declaimed the press agent in the manner of a circus barker, "was born in the shadow of the Sphinx, you know. It is very, very hot there, and she is cold!"

Pretending not to speak English, she sat there, pallid, languid, painfully polite, listening as the press agent answered the reporters' questions and assured them that Fox had discovered "the greatest living actress in the world." The atmosphere was redolent of tuberoses and incense.

She later admitted that she was hardly able to sustain the gag and that the instant the last of the press was gone she had torn off the stifling furs and thrown open the windows, yelling, "Gimme air!"

It is highly unlikely that the newspaper reporters were taken in by this charade, especially when one asked where she was born on the Nile and was answered with "the Left Bank." But Fox had calculated the degree of cheerful collusion in which reporters in search of a good story could be persuaded to indulge.

Louella Parsons' account of the presentation was published in her autobiography, *The Gay Illiterate*, in 1945. Apparently she repeated the tale in her *Los Angeles Herald-Examiner* column in July 1948, for Theda tried to spike it in a letter to *Los Angeles Times* columnist Hedda Hopper. On July 26 she concluded a long personal letter to her friend Hedda with the following:

> You've always been very *decent* to me, too: never made up yarns that humiliated me to make copy — as did recently the Lady on the other paper; and so utterly ridiculous!
>
> We came to California to make pictures, years ago, only, as everyone knows, in the winter, in order to take scenes that could not be filmed in the Eastern cold — and I certainly was entitled to wrap myself up in furs to avoid those biting blizzard winds in Chicago when we passed thro' en route to LA — even an Esquimo couldn't have taken it!
>
> If it were ever made an issue that Lady would perspire profusely in Chicago's zero-est weather trying to pull that fable out of the morgue — our first meeting was on the set in Fort Lee when I was making *Carmen*.

In the publicity campaign Theda Bara was touted as a reincarnation of the most evil women of the past, including Delilah and Lucrezia Borgia; she herself contributed to the legend by stating that in an earlier life she had been Egyptian, adding, "I remember crossing the Nile in barges to Karnak and Luxor as plainly as I recall crossing the Hudson Ferry today to come to the studio at Fort Lee."

Actually, she despised the notion of reincarnation, noting in 1919 that those who claimed to be reincarnated always recalled being Caesar or Napoleon, never part of the common herd. But it fit with Selig's nonsense, such as the prophecy he invented and claimed had been found in an ancient Egyptian tomb ("reported" by *Motion Picture Magazine* in April 1917):

> I, Thames, priest of Set, tell you this: She shall seem a snake to most men; she shall lead them to sin, and to their destruction. Yet she shall not be so. She shall be good and virtuous, and kind of heart; but she shall not seem so to most men. For she shall not be that which she appears! She shall be called Theta [the Greek letter θ].

In her later years Theda (or "Theta") admitted that she and her sister used to read these Selig and Goldfarb concoctions at breakfast and roar with laughter. "Some of them were so wild," she remembered, "we didn't think they would be printed, or that, if they were printed, they would be believed. But they were printed, all right, and they were believed, too, I suppose. The wildest press stories were the most successful ones. A lot of young ex-newspapermen wrote them. I think for a while I kept the whole publicity staff working nights."

Throughout the years Theda maintained a close relationship with her sister. Diane Kisro, one of the nurses at the Marycrest skilled nursing facility in Los Angeles, recalled how Lori had loved Theda, disliking the vamp image created for the latter and keeping a non-vamp photograph inscribed "To my Darling Little Twitter from Her Big Twitter."

Phony tales of her origins were so implanted by Fox's studio publicists, Johnny Goldfrap (whose name has also appeared as Goldfarb, Goldfrag, and Goldbrag) and Al Selig, that it is difficult to separate fact from fantasy. One of these silly fictions was that the name Theda Bara was an anagram for "Death Arab." The hard fact is that "Theda" came from "Theodosia" and that "Bara" came from a name in her maternal grandfather's family, Baranger. At any rate, Theodosia Goodman was no more; in her place for all time would be Theda Bara. Following her success, in 1917 all her family legally changed their names to Bara.

One new myth concerning her name change should be addressed at this point. Social historian Stephen Birmingham asserts that she changed her name to conceal her Jewishness. He points to other Russian and Polish Jews in Hollywood who underwent name changes because Jewish names would not look good in marquees: Jack Benny (Benjamin Kubelsky), Fanny Brice (Fanny Borach), Al Jolson (Asa Yoelson), Eddie Cantor (Isidor Iskowitch) and Sophie Tucker (Sonia Kalish), among many, many others. In fact, she never concealed her Jewish origins, as the interview with her old rabbi in 1915 and her own self-description as "just a nice Jewish girl…" in 1934 attest. The public, too, was well aware of her ethnic background, which became an issue when she portrayed Kathleen Mavourneen near the end of her career.

Within a few months the details of her origins were worked out, complete with contrived documentary records, and the world was told that Theda Bara was born in the Sahara in 1890, the daughter of Theda De Coppet, a French actress, and Giuseppe Bara, an Italian painter and sculptor. Her father was on a sketching tour in the great African desert, and his wife had accompanied him. "There," related columnist Archie Bell in November 1915, "amid the sand dunes, the waving palms and flashing steels in the belts of barbarous men, Theda Bara opened her eyes to the world — she believes that she has not lived since her death as Ar Minz, the gypsy smuggler of Cordova and Gibraltar, upon whose life and adventures Merimee based his life of 'Carmen.'" Weaned on serpents' blood, "a crystal-gazing seeress of profoundly occult powers," she came to films via stardom on the Paris stage, and spent her spare time driving men mad with love.

In 1916 she signed a cleverly written three-year contract with William Fox which had these eight provisions:

1. You cannot marry within three years;
2. You must be heavily veiled while in public;
3. You cannot take public transportation;
4. You cannot appear in the theater;
5. You cannot attend Turkish baths;
6. You cannot pose for snapshots;
7. You cannot close the curtains on the windows of your limousine;
8. You can only go out at night.

FOUR.
A Fool There Was

Who was Theda Bara? If there were any questions in the public mind, her role in *A Fool There Was* left no room for doubt.

A Fool There Was is a six-reeler that runs for a total of 58 minutes, 26 seconds, in which Theda Bara appears in about one-third of the frames. In it, happily married middle-aged family man and diplomat John Schuyler (played by Edward José), rich, influential and portly, learns that the president is sending him to Europe on a delicate mission of the utmost importance. The film opens with scenes of domestic happiness tinged with foreboding. The Vampire, inadvertently offended by Schuyler's wife, vows revenge upon her and sets her eyes on John Schuyler.

Theda is the vampire, a wicked woman who ruins honorable men by seducing them with her primitive, almost magical sexuality, then destroys the hapless creatures as they grovel at her feet with passion. Wearing Empire line dresses and occasionally a diadem with a stiff tuft of feathers, she does not do much languorous dallying, but pursues her victims with energy and strikes poses of regal triumph when they grovel. She is fashionably dressed, looking every bit the vampire with her deeply set dark eyes made up to look even darker, her already fair skin lightened to a pallor. As she heads for Schuyler's ship, a ragged, unshaven derelict stops her near the dock. This pathetic individual, a handsome young man just a year before, is one of her former lovers. The Vampire ensnared him, used him and tossed him aside. "See what you have made of me," he moans, "and still you prosper, you hellcat!"

On the voyage to Europe, diplomat and Vamp meet, not entirely by chance. He is hardly her match: "Kiss me, my fool!" she commands, and he does. At that moment, Schuyler's fate is sealed and a deathless American phrase is born. He surrenders, promptly vacates his quarters in favor of hers and makes her his life's sole interest, forgetting family and diplomatic assignment. To alert the audience that a seduction is taking place there are some scenes of arm-flinging and back-arching on Bara's part, and plenty of hard staring — unrecognizable today as any sort of come-hither look.

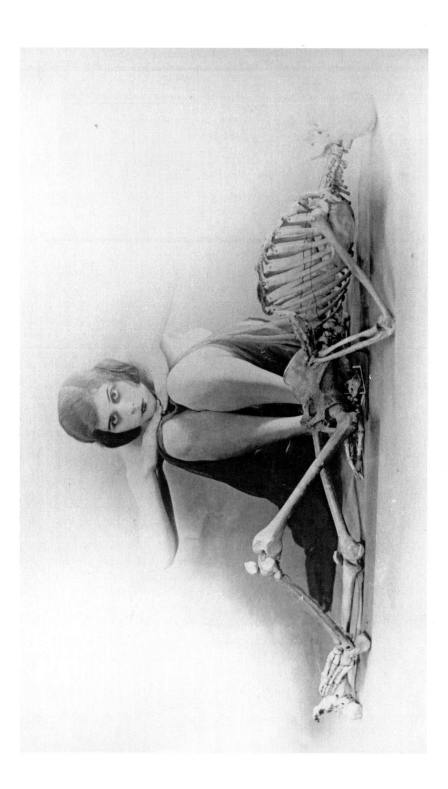

By the time the ship arrives in Europe, Schuyler has been reduced to an infatuated victim who dallies for two months on the Italian Riviera with the Vampire, becoming puffier and shakier with every scene. His family learns of his fall but is powerless to break the Vampire's spell from such a distance. Within another four months the Fool has been drained of wealth and pride, caring only for the Vamp and the whiskey bottle. The debauchery scenes show drunken couples waltzing together, lolling about in overstuffed chairs, packs of playing cards and empty whiskey bottles, fur coats lying where they were dropped, and chandeliers and tapestries dimly suggesting an orgy.

They return to New York where he rents a Fifth Avenue mansion for them. The Vamp leaves him for other men and fresh pastures; he stays in the mansion crawling across the thick carpeting in search of his bottle. Estranged from his family, dismissed by his government, ostracized by his former friends, Schuyler is nothing but a pathetic, bleary-eyed drooler in one scene. To heighten the sense of impending doom, director Powell here switches to a reddish-tinted film.

Remembering the man she loved, his wife attempts to reclaim him, and in a moment of conscience he vows to return to her and their child. But the Vamp returns, having heard that the Fool's wife plans to take him back, and utters her main line. "Kiss me, my fool," the Vamp cries, and he, drunken and dying, cannot resist her. He pats her cheek fondly and his wife runs distractedly out of the house.

This and another scene near the end of the film illustrate the way Theda snaps on her spell like a light switch. In the second attempt, the wife brings along their little girl to woo father back. She seems to be succeeding until the Vamp is observed slinking downstairs in a nightie, her hair cascading over her bare shoulders down to her waist. Instantly, the father breaks out of his child's arms, clutches the Vamp tightly and rests his head on her bosom with a blissful expression. As his tiny daughter is dragged away by her nearly fainting mother, pointing accusingly at her crazed father, the Vamp's eyes flash with victory. The Fool recalls the scenes of his earlier sins in a quick series of flashbacks, and he is then put out of his misery when he crawls deliriously through an open stair railing and plunges to his death on the floor of the vestibule below. The last title card reads: "So some of him lived, but the soul of him died."

In the final scene, Theda Bara stands triumphant in the vestibule, wearing a black velvet gown and a string of pearls and smiling wickedly as she holds a long-stemmed rose in her teeth and idly tosses rose petals onto the Fool's broken body. "Kiss me, my fool!" she mocks, taunting her expired lover to return to life. Then on the screen appears a Kiplingesque title:

Opposite: **A promotional photo for** *A Fool There Was* **(courtesy of the Academy of Motion Picture Arts and Sciences).**

The Fool Was Stripped
To His Foolish Hide.

The melodramatic formula, adhering to Edwardian era demands, called for scenes of wiles and resistance followed by seduction and familial grief. Debauchery, ostracism, bottle solace, and heart-rending pathos winding to the denouement of obliteration would follow in quick succession. The film's costumes and sets are all proper to 1914, and drinking and cards are the strongest symbols of evil. All of this was familiar to the audience.

Released in January 1915, *A Fool There Was* became a box office smash hit. Theda Bara's career of screen vamping was ordained and the English language gained "vamp" as a new word. According to Merriam Webster's Collegiate Dictionary, Tenth Edition, the noun (with a first usage date of 1911) meant "a woman who uses her charm or wiles to seduce and exploit men" while the verb (1915) meant "to practice seductive wiles on."

The critics responded favorably to the film. *Variety* reported that the "strong man caught in the meshes of the wicked woman makes an interesting theme. The life of the man and woman as shown in the picture during their time in Italy would make any fellow forget about the old home…. Miss Bara as the vampire scores easily. José did better when elderly. The remainder of the cast has been well chosen. The women are exceptionally attractive. Mabel Frenyear as the wife impresses, and May Allison [1895–1989] as the sister is petite and attractive. In direction the picture has been well taken care of. A bit of mixed-up business enters when the characters are said to be in Italy in one instance, and again in London. Explanation would have removed all doubt as to who kept up the beautiful home while the husband was away with the other woman. The scene in the vampire's apartment at the ending of the picture is rather broad."

Typical of the difficulties faced by filmmakers, the crew had gone to Florida to take advantage of its sunny climate for some bathing suit shots. The temperature turned out to be 40 degrees, and when the scene was shot the censors would not allow it to be used anyway. Apparently the chilliness had had an effect on the swimsuit-clad women that was unmaskable in the days before airbrushing.

Not only was Theda's career guaranteed, but so was the future of the Fox Studio. This film and her later ones gave Fox its eminence in the motion picture world. Powell had cast her under the name "Theda Bara" in what was intended to be a subordinate role to the presumed star, Edward José, a 34-year-old who was also a newcomer to films. The sultry Theda with her imperious "Kiss me, my fool!" stole the show. When Fox learned that all over the country exhibitors were billing her name above José's, he signed her to a five-year starring contract, supplemented by the 1916 agreement.

A Fool There Was gave Theda an opportunity for "deep breathing, hungry sighing and smoldering eye-work," as the *Los Angeles Mirror* recounted years later. Thrilled by her diabolical enchantment, the entire country, which had been hyped by Fox's promotional campaign of the debut of this reincarnation of every evil woman since the dawn of time, was sitting on the edge of theater chairs.

Miriam Cooper, wife of director Raoul Walsh (1887–1980), despised Theda Bara, and the dislike was reciprocated. In her opinion, Theda "was terrible. Her only expression was to duck her head and stare at the leading man or camera with what appeared to be a searching look…. She was … nearsighted, … overweight, coarse and unattractive, entirely different from the slender young Griffith girls…. But in her stage makeup she looked exotic and sultry."

For their part, *Los Angeles*

A 1916 publicity photo (courtesy UCLA Arts Library, Special Collections).

Times readers may have sympathized with Theda, who was quoted as saying she "cried for two days and lost 14 pounds over having to appear in a one-piece bathing suit" in the movie. But W. C. Fields ridiculed her as "Molta Zitkrantz Bara, A Vampire" in *The Mountain Sweep Stakes* (1919), one of several melodrama parodies he wrote. In the Fields version there is a scene in which ice cream is delivered to "Lew 'Left-Foot' Chaplin" ("A Wag") and Bara, with the former spilling some into his trousers. But in trying to shake it down his pant leg without distracting Bara, he drops the ice cream through both his pants and the floor grating underneath so that it ends up on the back of "Blaha Dressler" ("Still in the Ring"), who is seated below them.

Contemporary audiences might laugh at *Fool*'s satanic heroine and her evil power over her victims, but the audiences who saw it in 1915 were enthralled. Unsophisticated as they were as film viewers, it is easy to understand the impact of this publicity-created star, for the Goldfarb-Selig campaign that preceded the film was really the exposition of the character Theda Bara plays in it. Filmgoers believed what they saw. Film historian Alex Walker wrote that "her mesmeric malevolence has neither rational nor supernatural motivation." To that generation of melodrama-weaned filmgoers — many of whom still lit their homes with kerosene lamps, though they were familiar with the electric lights downtown — Bara's power needed no explanation. Seeing was believing.

FIVE

A Film a Month

Films of 1915

*H*aving secured her by a contract, Fox proceeded to work Theda as hard as he could, turning out at one point an average of a film a month. In the four-year period after *A Fool There Was*, Theda appeared in 38 films. Eight were made in 1915: *The Kreutzer Sonata, The Clemenceau Case, The Devil's Daughter, Lady Audley's Secret, The Two Orphans, Sin, Carmen* and *The Galley Slave*.

The Kreutzer Sonata, a Russian tragedy based on Jacob Gordon's play version of Count Leo Tolstoy's sexually autobiographical short story, was directed by Herbert Brenon (1880-1958). Opposite Nance O'Neil and William E. Shay, Theda played Esther Rusoff, a wicked adulteress murdered by the sister she betrayed, and was billed as "The Woman of 1000 Faces." Exhibitors and audiences who had responded to Theda's uniqueness in *A Fool There Was* agreed that she was the real selling point of *The Kreutzer Sonata*.

Of her second role and its reception she later said; "When I found myself cast in my second picture in support of an artist, I felt only an ambition to do as well as she did. When the picture was released there were indications that I had done well. Exhibitors wrote me that my name had been the drawing feature. It is a name, therefore, that has some emotional value in a world in which romance is a food all hearts crave."

The Clemenceau Case, a domestic tragedy in which wicked wife Theda is slain by the husband she has wronged, was also directed by Brenon and was taken from Martha Woodson's adaptation of an Alexandre Dumas novel. Starring with Shay, Stuart Holmes (1887–1971), Jane Lee and Mrs. Cecil Raleigh, Theda Bara received her first real star billing, with her name in large letters above the title.

Dumas had long been fascinated by the vampire and *femme fatale* roles, devoting as he did five chapters in his *Mémoirs* to a discussion of an 1820s Parisian play, *Le vampire, mélodrame en trois actes avec un prologue*. But had

A 1916 photo that appeared in a newspaper sup-
plement (courtesy of the Academy of Motion Picture Arts and Sciences).

Dumas lived to see Theda's version he would have loudly argued for creative control over a film.

A Syracuse, New York, reviewer described *The Clemenceau Case* as the tale of a "devil woman, lasciviously appealing, whose aim in life is to ruin her admirers, the artistic chap who falls victim to her lust, the rival, who is killed, the friend, the friend's wife and the friend's child to add pathos; the artist's dying mother, the final scenes in which to save the friend the artist murders the woman and gives himself up to the police." He concluded, ominously, "it cannot, of course, be recommended for people of high school age." Who knew what evil tendencies it might unleash in a preadult mind?

In this vein, *The Dramatic Mirror* questioned whether any "wholly pure minded man or woman could take a great deal of pleasure in witnessing such an exposition of female depravity." The reviewer noted that to *read* such works by a "great master" was a far cry from "seeing it acted out on the screen with all the hue of a beautiful passionate woman to increase sensual appeal. After seeing a picture of this kind one is tempted to ask, 'Where is the National Board of Censorship?'"

According to the *Louisville Herald*, Bara developed a "peculiar serpentine walk" (which the writer also described as "pantherish") especially for her role in *The Clemenceau Case*. The walk "lithe, sinuous [and] characteristic of the vampire-woman"—was reportedly taught to Bara by her "warm friend" Isadora Duncan (1878–1927). Whether or not this was true, Isadora Duncan's name certainly achieved Fox's goal of maximum publicity. Isadora, to the average American, was a scandalous woman of questionable morals and indiscreet affairs. Her association, genuine or not, with La Bara would be just the ticket to heighten the seductive image.

The Devil's Daughter, another dramatic tragedy, was filmed in Florida. Directed by Frank Powell, it was based on Garfield Thompson's translation of a Gabriele D'Annunzio play. Fox, rarely concerned with the truth if it conflicted with the making of a dollar, reported that the Italian poet had written the part for Eleanora Duse, but decided to give it to Theda after seeing her in *The Clemenceau Case.* Playing opposite Paul Doucet (1886–1928), Victor Benoit, Robert Wayne, Jane Lee, Jane Miller and Doris Heywood, Theda played the wicked Cavalina, known as "La Giaconda," the central character of the original play — "an even more ruthless siren than in any of her [earlier] dramas."

Lady Audley's Secret, still another dramatic tragedy, was directed by Marshall Farnum and came from a novel and play by Miss M. E. Braddon. The other stars were Clifford Bruce, William Riley Hatch, Stephen Gratten and Warner Richmond. Theda Bara, billed as "the most wickedly beautiful face in the entire world," played the evil Lady Audley, whose secret is the murder she has committed.

As her fame and bank account grew, Bara requested, then demanded, roles other than those of vamps. So Fox grumblingly gave her the lead in *The Two Orphans*, a romance filmed in Quebec about two beautiful orphan sisters in *ancien régime* France. Theda played Henriette, who protects her blind sister Louise. Fox knew that the extra cost of moving to Quebec was worth it, since it allowed a celebrity-hungry fringe area a chance to have a closer look at the divinely diabolical temptress. Brenon directed the film from a play by Andolphe D'Ennery. The other stars were Brenon himself, Shay, Jean Southern, Gertrude Berkley, Frank Goldsmith, E. L. Fernandez, Sheridan Block, Mrs. Cecil Raleigh and John D. Murphy. The play's theatrical power was regarded as "unquestionable" by several critics — one called it "quite without literary quality"— and it was considered a thing of amazement that Theda Bara, "of all people," would star in the film version. It had already been filmed at Selig, with Kathryn Williams in the role of Henriette, and it would later appear with Lillian Gish as D. W. Griffith's *Orphans of the Storm*.

Bara's public was disappointed because their vamp had suddenly gone noble. Actually, at least half of her roles were more sympathetic than vampirish. Fox, however, foxily used her vampire image in most of the films, and audiences came to read evil meanings into her most innocent actions. Though apparently unhappy with her vamp roles, in late 1917 Theda announced to her public, "During the rest of my screen career, I am going to continue doing vampires as long as people sin. For I believe that humanity needs the moral lesson and it needs it in repeatedly large doses."

When she wrote a screenplay of her own for Fox, *The Soul of Buddha*, in 1918, she created a cunning little Oriental vamp to be portrayed, of course, by herself. She was well aware that her public wanted her to sneer at virtue, to clad herself in the scantiest of costly attire and lure all types of good men to their destruction. Some critics, however, were tiring of the vamp roles as early as May 1916. The *New York Times* commented that Theda's cleverness was "proven by the fact that she burst from obscurity into fame when her first picture appeared.... But she has vampired so much that she has lost her sense of values and caricatures a type of woman she formerly gave a vivid portrait of. Now accumulation of detail and over-emphasis have spoiled the portrait. The fault is really the director's for making her repeat so often a thing that was exaggerated in the beginning."

Sin, in which Theda was billed as "Destiny's Dark Angel," was a dramatic tragedy directed by Brenon from a play by Nixola Daniels. Bara played the Italian peasant girl Cora; her co-stars were William E. Shay, Warner Oland (1880-1938), Mrs. Louise Rial and Henry Leone.

Cora forsakes her peasant sweetheart for an Americanized Italian, Pietro, who takes her to New York's Little Italy. There a villain, Luigi, sees her and, jealous of Pietro, promises to steal the sacred jewels from a statue of the Madonna. Cora promises her heart "to such a man and to such a man only," and Luigi removes the jewels from the Madonna. As that moment the chapel bell rings and a shout is heard as the robbery is discovered. Luigi lays the jewels before Cora and "she becomes insane at the enormity of the crime, alternately laughing and crying," according to the *Chicago Daily News*, which headlined its review, "Theda Bara has a play that fits her."

Bara's next film, *Carmen*, was a dramatic tragedy in which she played the gypsy temptress. Directed by Raoul Walsh from Prosper Mérimée's novel, the film also starred Einar Linden, Carl Harbaugh, James Marcus, Elsie MacLeod, Fay Tunis and Emil de Varny. At the same time the Fox-Bara *Carmen* was filmed and released, Cecil B. DeMille was directing his version with the movie debut of Geraldine Farrar (1882–1967), an opera diva with the New York Metropolitan. (Her vocal talent was wasted, for the film antedated sound in movies by a dozen years.) At the same time that Fox and DeMille were releasing their versions, Charlie Chaplin (1889–1977) released his burlesque of both the opera and the two film productions. Fox had hoped to open before the DeMille production, but the releases were simultaneous. Thus did the *Cleveland Ledger* proclaim with a headline: "Theda Bara to Appear in Carmen: Movies' Biggest Battle Is Near."

Fox's *Carmen* was one of the first pre–Hollywood film epics. Production costs totaled $200,000, with the city of Cordova being reproduced at Fort Lee. There were 5,000 extras, a real bullfight and daredevil Art Jarvis, "who makes an 83 foot leap with a horse from a cliff into deep water" according to the Louisville reviewer, who was one among the "immense crowds at the Mary Anderson" theater in his city who voted Theda Bara "the ideal Carmen."

Theda was praised, but the real kudos went to diva Farrar. The *Motion Picture News* said of Theda's Carmen: "It has all the vampire's fierceness when aroused, but a depth of will power and of mystery that a vampire could never have." The *New York Times* credited the Fox production as "an example of excellent motion picture photography, but its scenario ... is loose and vague, and Miss Bara seems very mechanically seductive...." *Photoplay* gushed, "Was not Carmen a vampire? And is there the slightest doubt about Theda Bara being a vampire?... Madame Bara — as was her prerogative — had

A still from the smoking scene in *Carmen* (courtesy of the Academy of Motion Picture Arts and Sciences).

her own ideas about Carmen — ideas which, to say the least, gave piquancy to the role. Hers was the most modern Carmen we have had. No traditions for La Bara! No paltry conventions of the operatic stage to cramp her style! She even smoked modern, machine-made Turkish cigarettes...." The *Philadelphia Press* spoke of her "wonderful mobility of countenance" and her "striking portrayal" of the "fateful cigarette girl of Seville." The *Springfield Union* described Theda's Carmen as "not over-refined [but never giving] a suggestion of unnecessary coarseness."

Later Pola Negri was Carmen for Lubitsch, known in America as *Gypsy Love*, while other actresses such as Dolores Del Rio (1908–1983), Vivian Romance, Rita Hayworth and Dorothy Dandridge (1923–1965) have all scored in their versions of *Carmen*, as did Raquel Meller in 1926, Imperio Argentina in 1938, and Julia Mignes Johnson in Francesco Rossi's 1984 version.

Of her role in *Carmen* Theda later wrote,

> I remember being costumed for the character of Carmen in the conventional splendor of a prima-donna. I looked well enough, and, as I appeared for the scene, there were complimentary expressions of approval by the rest of the company, but I was not happy with the clothes. I knew that Carmen

herself would have resented them. They were the traditional prettiness of the operatic heroine, dressed for grand opera. I hated them. I went back to my dressing-room and got hold of an old piece of rose-velvet brocade that had been used for upholstery. I raveled up the surface with a nail file till it looked worn, shabby, a bit of frazzled finery. This I made quickly into a skirt. I found an old, sleeveless muslin waist. Added to the entire effect, I wore some glass beads, ear-rings, a Spanish comb, and then I coarsened my features in make-up to give to the face that defiant challenge of Carmen, the factory girl.

This was the kind of girl I had become, inwardly, and I succeeded in looking like her outwardly. In the fight scene with one of the factory girls they selected a robust, thick-ankled, solid sort of woman from the tenement districts, a real type, picked to make a real fight with me. I took a violent personal dislike to her, as I watched her for days before the scene was played. She was told to kill me, if necessary, and I was warned to actually defend myself. Realism in the movies is so essential that one loses one's temper over it, sometimes. I did so on this occasion. It was a real fight. We pulled hair, we scratched, we wrestled, we tumbled over and under one another in the best artistic movie form. When it was over, I was covered with bruises, but the other girl had fainted — not I.

And what of the competing versions of *Carmen*? The *New York Telegraph* compared the two lead actresses guardedly, perhaps not wishing to provoke Theda's screen anger: "Miss Bara's version of the emotional heroine of the Spanish [*sic*] story is a somewhat different one from that of Miss Farrar's, but it is quite as satisfactory in every respect. Miss Farrar's acting is more abandoned in parts than Miss Bara's, but the latter gives a strong, finished performance throughout, and the shades of emotionalism are only a matter of opinion."

The Galley Slave, another tragedy, this time of revenge, saw Theda Bara again billed as "Destiny's Dark Angel," and was directed by J. Gordon Edwards from Bartley Campbell's play. It was the story of the deserted wife of a young artist. With Stuart Holmes, Claire Whitney and Jane Lee, Bara played the wronged wife seeking revenge in her final film of 1915.

Films of 1916

In 1916 she starred in nine more films: *Destruction, The Serpent, Gold and the Woman, The Eternal Sapho, East Lynne, Under Two Flags, Her Double Life, Romeo and Juliet* and *The Vixen*.

Destruction was a melodramatic tragedy directed by Will S. Davis from his own story. The other actors were Joseph Furny, Esther Hoier, Warner Oland, J. Herbert Frank, Carleton Macy, Frank Evans and Gaston Bell. A large advertisement announced, "The most famous vampire in her most daring role brings ruin and disaster to thousands." Theda played an evil woman who not only seeks to destroy a father and son, but nearly wrecks an entire town by inciting a strike.

The Serpent was melodramatic tragedy in which she played Vania Lazar, a Russian peasant who seeks revenge on the duke who wronged her, and through him revenge on all men; the revenge is realized only in a dream, however. Directed by Raoul Walsh from a story by Philip Bartholomae, the film also featured George Walsh (1892–1981), James Marcus, Lillian Hathaway, Charles Craig and Carl Harbaugh.

Generally the critics were not kind to this film, with one (cited by Hamilton) writing that "Theda is rather a sneering heroine... making frequent use of the curling lip and wicked eye." But the *New York Times* reviewer felt that "the little touches that go to make [the film] above the average of its kind.... is real[ism].... Miss Bara's following is easily accounted for by this picture. She is a clever actress with a high sense of screen values. Hers is a marvelously mobile and expressive face that can express deeper scorn by the curl of the lip or greater sorrow through an expression of her eyes than the average screen player can denote with exaggerated heavings and writhings." The *Los Angeles Examiner*'s reviewer described the film as "thrilling, different, and intensely interesting throughout, containing a happy mixture of tragedy, pathos, romance and comedy."

A domestic insight into the filming of *The Serpent* was provided by Miriam Cooper, newly wed to Bara's director Raoul Walsh. Theda insisted on staying in New York, which necessitated a slow ferry crossing of the icy Hudson River to the studio at Fort Lee. Walsh was frustrated by interminable, expensive delays, and nightly returned home in a bad mood from ferry rides and from directing Theda, who irritated Miriam no end by "mooing" (making cow eyes) at Raoul. But at the end of the filming, Fox saw the practicality of a California studio and made his move. Theda had to go along.

Gold and the Woman was a revenge tragedy, in which Bara played Theresa DeCordova, a woman who has been wronged and forces a venal English colonel to pay. The climactic scene has her, the daughter of a Mexican aristocrat, donning a suit of armor in her ancestral halls when revolutionaries attack the hacienda and departing in this getup with the bandits, lined up on either side, gaping at this strange apparition. Directed by James Vincent from a story by Daniel Roosevelt, the film also starred H. Cooper Cliffe, Alma Hanlon, Harry Hilliard, Caroline Harris, Ted Griffin, Louis Stern, James Sheehan, Carleton Macy, Frank Whitson and Pauline Barry.

Of this film the *New York Times* critic was friendly and sympathetic: the movie "again displayed Theda Bara's opulent beauty on the screen," but her talents were wasted "in the absurdities of [the movie's] incidents [which] surpass[ed] the fantastic hallucinations of a lotus eater." On the other hand, the

A studio publicity shot of Theda with her favorite hound (courtesy of the Academy of Motion Picture Arts and Sciences).

Cleveland Plain Dealer's critic opined that there could be no sympathy for Theda Bara. "Among the nice things Theda does in her latest film is to beguile an old soldier from the path of rectitude, compromise the hero, compel her lover to marry his ward and then live a life of sin with the husband under the same roof as the blind wife."

In the last scene the vampire transforms into Satan amid "the red glow and sulfuric vapor." The *Plain Dealer's* critic described the overall effect as "a glut of vice and an orgy of wickedness hitherto unattained even by the notorious Fox vampire."

The Eternal Sapho was a romantic tragedy directed by Bertram Bracken from Alphonse Daudet's "Sapho." With Warner Oland, Frank Norcross, George MacQuarrie, Walter Lewis, Hattie Delano, James Cooley, Einar Linden, Mary Martin and Kittens Reichert, Theda played Moya Wilson, the artist's model. The film's climax allowed the artistic touch of Theda melting into a statue representing the symbol of her own downfall.

South Carolina's *Columbia Citizen*, under the headline "Theda Bara is Up to Old Tricks in Revised Sapho," accused her of using the film to "make goo-goo eyes, to twist her lips into the familiar sneer, to wear emotional clothes and to heave her chest violently." But a kinder critic at the *Cleveland Plain Dealer* wrote that she "is a vampire again, to be sure, but this time not a deliberate cold blooded one. She is driven by fate from one to another, and she wrecks the lives of the men who come into contact with her. But she does not mean to do it. You will not hate this Theda Bara, and for the most part you will sympathize with her. Nay, perhaps like her." A vampire with a conscience?

East Lynne, another romantic tragedy, in which Theda played Lady Isabel Carlisle, was directed by Bertram Bracken from Mrs. Henry Wood's novel and play. Lady Isabel runs off with a murderer and ultimately poses as a nurse to be with her dying child. The other stars were Claire Whitney, Stuart Holmes, William Tooker and Stanhope Wheatcroft. Later Fox made two new versions, with Alma Rubens in the lead and then as an early talkie with Ann Harding (1904-1981). Three years before Theda's version it had been the first six-reeler British film. Audiences had trouble identifying the vamp with the long-suffering Lady Audley. When Fox moved the story's setting from the nineteenth century to the present the villainy seemed almost tame by the audiences' standards.

Under Two Flags, in which Theda played Cigarette, was a drama about the French Foreign Legion directed by J. Gordon Edwards from a novel by Ouida. The other performers were Holmes, Whitney and Herbert Heyes. In a later silent version by Universal, Priscilla Dean starred, and still later 20th Century–Fox made a talkie with Claudette Colbert (1903–) in Theda's old role. Heyes' son, Douglas, recalled the plot: "Seems dad had struck a superior (but rotten) officer and was booked to be shot at sunrise, when — I have it here in dad's crumbling scrapbook, in a yellowed trade-paper review of Thursday, August 3, 1916: '...she arrives with the reprieve at the last moment, riding in with the papers in her hand just as the shot is fired. She is killed by the bullets intended for the man she loved and dies in his arms, while kissing the flag of France.' Such decency," he concluded, "was rare for Miss Bara."

Another fan was a "Daddy" Camp, a resident of New York City's Home for Old Men and Aged Couples. He played a minor role in the movie and was kissed several times by Theda Bara in it. Evidently he never recovered, for his dying wish was to see her again, closing his eyes after looking at "a photograph of the vampire and [begging] that Miss Bara attend his funeral. Incidentally," the *Cleveland Leader* reported, "she sent a beautiful tribute to the last rites." Her publicist, never averse to additional publicity, added a note of her latest film playing at a downtown theater.

Her Double Life was a melodrama also directed by J. Gordon Edwards from a story by the script writer, Mary Murillo, who created four other Theda Bara scripts. Theda's costars were Holmes, Lee, Walter Law and Lucia Moore. She played Mary Doone, a Red Cross nurse who poses as an English noblewoman. The *New York Times* critic was unimpressed; writing of this movie's title, he felt that it was "seven lives less than Theda Bara is usually called upon to live in the course of five reels."

Romeo and Juliet, directed by Edwards from Shakespeare's play, had Theda as Juliet. The other stars were Harry Hilliard, Glen White, Walter Law, Einar Linden, Jane Lee and her sister Katherine, John W. Dillon, Edwin Eaton, Edwin Holt, Alice Gale, Victory Bateman and Helen Tracy. "William Shakespeare Fox," according to the *New York Times*, had changed the story's end so that even the Bard would approve, having Juliet upon waking from her coma discover "Romeo and being overjoyed when he tells her that he has come to take her away to Mantua. But her joy is short-lived for she learns in a moment that he has taken poison and death is upon him, so she kills herself. The result from this is the same, of course, but the brief colloquy between the lovers shrouds the play in still deeper gloom...."

Theda's Juliet was as highly praised as Beverly Bayne's, in a film made and released simultaneously and expensively by Metro, in which Romeo was played by Francis X. Bushman. Both pictures were praised equally and Theda's Juliet was called "a signal triumph of versatility." A sympathetic trade reviewer wrote of Theda, "She is young and her long dark curls made many a beautiful picture as she enacts ... the fairest girl in all Verona."

"As Juliet," she recalled, "I was again pursued with accusations of presenting a vampire-Juliet. I gave the character a great deal of study, and perhaps in that investigation discovered that Juliet lived in a period of passionate abandon. Italy, in the days of Romeo and Juliet, was no place for a Sunday-school girl. I did assume that Juliet, in spite of her youth, was a glowing beauty of that most romantic of Italian periods."

Like the two *Carmen*s, the two *Romeo and Juliet*s made nothing but money. In the talking era, the most famous Juliets have been Norma Shearer, with Leslie Howard (1890–1943) as her Romeo in George Cukor's M-G-M production; Susan Shentall, with Laurence Harvey (1928–1973) as Romeo in the Universal-Ciné Company version shot in Italy and directed by Renato

Castellani in 1954, with Technicolor; and Franco Zeffirelli's beautiful color version made in 1968 with Olivia Hussey (1953-) as Juliet and Edward Whiting as Romeo.

The Vixen was a melodrama directed by J. Gordon Edwards, in which Theda played Elsie Drummond, the wicked sister who nearly ruins her good sister's life. The other performers were Mary Martin, Herbert Heyes, A. H. Van Buren, George Clarke, Carl Gerard and George Odell.

Films of 1917

In 1917 Theda Bara appeared in eight more films: *The Darling of Paris, The Tiger Woman, Her Greatest Love, Heart and Soul, Camille, Cleopatra, The Rose of Blood* and *Madame DuBarry.*

The Darling of Paris was a French medieval romance directed by Edwards and based on Victor Hugo's *The Hunchback of Notre Dame.* As Esmeralda, the wild gypsy girl, Theda costarred with Glen White, Walter Law, Herbert Heyes, Carey Lee, Alice Gale, John Webb Dillon and Louis Dean. In this unique version, Quasimodo is a handsome knight who rescues Esmeralda from the torture rack, not an ugly hunchback. In 1923 Universal made a silent spectacle with Patsy Ruth Miller as Esmeralda to Lon Chaney's brilliant Quasimodo; in talking versions, Maureen O'Sullivan (1911-) and Charles Laughton (1899–1962) were the stars of RKO's 1939 version, and Gina Lollobrigida (1927–) and Anthony Quinn (1915–) played the roles in the 1957 film.

The Tiger Woman, a melodramatic tragedy again directed by J. Gordon Edwards, was based on a story by James Adams. Theda Bara played a Russian villainess, the Countess Irma, who becomes the ruthless Princess Petrovich. Committing every sort of crime, she is eventually hanged for her evildoing. Billed as "The Champion Vampire of the Season," Theda was flanked by White, Dillon, Dean, Heyes, Mary Martin, Emil de Varny, Edwin Holt, Florence Martin, Kate Blanke and Kittens Reichert.

Her Greatest Love was a romantic drama in which Bara was again directed by Edwards. It was based on a novel by Ouida. Theda's costars were White, Gale, Harry Hilliard, Walter Law and Marie Curtis. Theda played Hazel, who having fallen victim to a brutal husband in a forced marriage, chooses to go to Siberia to redeem her soul. *Moving Picture World* felt that "she is not the right type, to begin with, and her assumption of girlish innocence, in the earlier scenes, is set at naught by the eyes and mouth that have done so much to assure her standing as one of the leading vampires of the screen."

Heart and Soul was a romantic tragedy of the Hawaiian Islands, in which Theda played Jess, who sacrifices her life for the man she loves. It was directed by Edwards, as were her previous seven and following 14 pictures, and was

The original caption for this promotional shot for *Cleopatra* read, "Theda Bara, inventor of vamping, is coming back into the movies to show some of these upstarts how to crush a man's soul" (courtesy UCLA Arts Library, Special Collections).

based on Sir Rider Haggard's *Jess*, originally set in Africa. The other actors were Hilliard, White, Whitney, Law, Dillon and Edwin Holt.

Of J. Gordon Edwards (1885–1925), grandfather of Blake Edwards, Theda said: "[He] was kind and considerate and the nicest director I ever had. Some directors are wonderful. They give you such funny advice on manners and deportment. One time I asked my director about a certain scene. 'Do I repulse the advances of this man or do I lead him on?' I asked. The director was stumped. He hadn't an idea of what to do. Finally he hit upon a lively answer. 'Oh, just keep the audience guessing,' he said."

Camille, a romantic tragedy based on a Dumas, *fils,* novel and play, starred Bara in the title role. The movie was advertised as "A Masterpiece of Bara Art — A Theda Bara Super Picture." The other stars were Law, White, Gale, Whitney and Albert Roscoe. Another version by a rival company, starring Helen Hesperia, was released simultaneously, with Theda's garnering greater praise. (Later Bara quipped that "it might not be particularly interesting to the reader to be told that I have played Camille.") Other Camilles of the silents included Sarah Bernhardt, Clara Kimball Young, Nazimova (1879–1945) and Norma Talmadge; there were two French talkies, the first in 1935 with Yvonne Printemps and another in 1969 with Daniele Gaubert. The definitive version, however, is Greta Garbo's 1937 for George Cukor of M-G-M.

Cleopatra, the longest of Theda's films (eleven reels, as compared to an average of six) and one of the biggest money-makers, was a historical romance based on Shakespeare, Sardou and historical works. The Fox production cost half a million dollars, had a cast of 30,000, and included the Roman Forum, Alexandria, the desert, pyramids and Sphinx, the sea battle of Actium; and the battle of Alexandria. The script was created by Adrian Johnson, who worked on 13 Theda Bara films, including some prior to *Cleopatra*. Theda, of course, played the Egyptian queen, while other roles were assigned to Fritz Leiber, Thurston Hall, Albert Roscoe, Genevieve Blinn, Henri de Vries, Dorothy Drake, Dell Duncan, Hector Sarno, Herschel Mayall and Art Acord (1890–1931).

There was no research department at the studio so Theda, by her own account, "worked for months with the curator of Egyptology at the Metropolitan Museum in New York." The exteriors were shot in California, but part of the film was shot in New Jersey.

Alice Brown, in the *Columbus* (Ohio) *Journal,* wrote that the film opened with a shot of the desert "stretching out illimitably, with the Sphinx in the distance. Then we come closer to the Sphinx until at last there is a close-up of the enigmatic lady, and lo! her face is that of Theda Bara, who opens her eyes, twists her mouth and raises one brow in the manner familiar to film fans."

The film displayed more of Theda's shoulders — with over 30 changes of costumes, consisting mostly of beads — than the film censors appreciated. The exposure of flesh caused a furor, causing the Better Films Committee of the Women's Club of Omaha to condemn the movie in what was described as the most exciting meeting the group ever had. Theda Bara filed a $100,000 suit against the Chicago censor for refusing to give the picture a permit. Of course, the film was booked solid, and made a million dollars. This fantastically successful movie (77,000 saw it in New York alone, where it played 11 weeks) received this typical compliment from the *New York Review*: "Proud, defiant, willful, emotional, sinuous by turns, Miss Bara makes a representation the most auspiciously successful in her career."

Other critics were not so kind. Striking perhaps a patriotic note in the shortage days of World War I, Richard Stokes, in the *St. Louis Post-Dispatch*, sniffed that the movie was a vast "waste of rich resources." The *Cleveland Press*'s reviewer found that in the picture "Caesar and Cleopatra are posturing and raving even when they are alone, and pose as stiffly as a citizen in a boiled shirt before the camera of the village photographer." He also noted, uncharitably, that Theda's "appearance doesn't change although during the picture Cleopatra ages from 17 to 39 or 40." The *Brooklyn Eagle* made even more unkind observations: "She makes a burlesque of the serpent of the Nile, and is never for one moment convincing. She could never tempt a man to be late for dinner, much less to give up the throne of Rome. When she was not repulsive, she was funny."

On the subject of her dress, or lack of it, the *Plain Dealer* declared that "Of all the Vampires of Screen There's None So Bare as Theda," and the *Cleveland Leader*'s reviewer noted unkindly — as did critics of Elizabeth Taylor's 1963 version — that the brief costumes showed that the vamp had been gaining weight and perhaps should change her name to "Feeda Bara." The Springfield newspaper accused her of substituting "a low-cut gown for any attempt at clever acting ... doing odd sorts of squirms ... instead of trying to portray seductiveness."

Mrs. E. Schiefelin of Los Angeles recalled that the *Cleopatra* costume created quite a stir because it cost $1,000 a yard and Theda seemed to be wearing only ten cents' worth. After the film was released a reporter asked Theda where she had been born and the Vamp Queen responded, "Two blocks from the Sphinx."

Louella Parsons, writing in the *Chicago Herald* in September 1917, offered her sympathy to the ancient queen, a "poor lady, resting in her queenly tomb. All these ages and ages, she had little idea her system of vamping the men of her time would pass down through the centuries and be preserved in the moving pictures by filmland's chief vampire."

The *New York Times* called it "an uncommonly fine picture," despite the various negative remarks from other quarters. The performance was hard to top.

The rest of her screen career was downhill.

One of the scandalously brief costumes from *Cleopatra* (courtesy of the Academy of Motion Picture Arts and Sciences).

Bara commented on the blockbuster in 1919:

My most interesting character, to my mind, has been Cleopatra. She was a woman of immortal pride. She, too, must be labeled vampire, on that account. I do not think she was, in spite of the opinion of movie fans. The vampire after all may be the return to earth of Venus, in one of her myriad

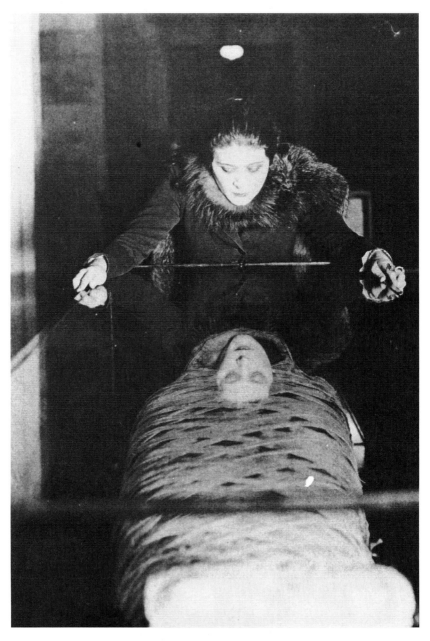

In a promotional shot for *Cleopatra*, Bara looks at her reflection in a mummy case at the Museum of Egyptology in New York (courtesy UCLA Arts Library, Special Collections).

disguises. In *Cleopatra* the disguise is not so modern. I have interpreted Venus in such modern disguises that have reminded me we are living in a practical age. When I have read about myself as a "celebrated vampire," the term has become as pungently commercial to my mind as omega oil. Today it has become a greater stench in my cinematograph nostrils. It was in *Cleopatra* that, under temperamental impulse, I thrashed a man so that he ran away. He was an Italian, playing the part of Mark Antony's messenger. In the scene of Cleopatra's rage, I had to beat him. He ran away before I could kill him, and the director called him back. He rushed up, trembling, and said to the director, "just look at my back." There were cuts upon him, it was bleeding.I looked at it myself, in amazement. Probably the rings or jewels I was wearing had scratched his skin. I was not conscious of my own strength. Of course, it was not strength at all, it was the emotional expression of Cleopatra's rage.

Historically, this was a celebrated picture, because of its infinite detail, if nothing else. I was told by one director that my walk in *Cleopatra* was one of immortal pride. He asked me if it had been cut out of the film. It had not, but my brother told me that the reason he didn't see it was because he fell asleep during the picture. Such is the humbug of directors.

The picture was road-shown in its initial engagements, and a symphony orchestra, supplemented in each city by the best local musicians, traveled with the print. Other famous Cleopatras have been Claudette Colbert (for DeMille), Vivian Leigh (in Shaw's *Caesar and Cleopatra*) and Elizabeth Taylor (for 20th Century–Fox).

From Bara to Taylor, every Cleopatra has had the same hairstyle, a pageboy bob with bangs. Actually, Egyptian ladies of Cleopatra's time shaved their heads and wore wigs stiffly molded with fat and glue, in appearance somewhat akin to the Cleopatra hairstyle launched by Theda.

Art Acord, who played one of Cleopatra's Egyptian attendants, was in the movies until the talkies revealed his high-pitched voice. He subsequently and briefly became a gold miner and finally committed suicide in a cheap Mexican hotel.

The Rose of Blood, a melodrama of revenge, had Theda playing Lisza Tapenka, a Russian revolutionary who loves Russia better than the men she loves and kills. It was based on a story by Richard Ordynski, who also starred in the movie, along with Charles Clary, Herschel Mayall, Marie Kiernan, Bert Turner, Genevieve Blinn, Joe King and Hector Sarno.

Madame DuBarry, from a Dumas novel, was a historical drama of the times of Louis XV and the French Revolution. Theda was Jeanne Vaubernier, a milliner's assistant who becomes Madame Du Barry, the king's mistress. For the only time in her screen career, Theda became a blonde for the sake of historical accuracy. The other stars were Charles Clary, Herschel Mayall, Fred Church, Genevieve Blinn and Willard Louis. The greatest Du Barry of all was

This still from *Madame DuBarry* is unusual in two ways: it shows Theda Bara blonde for the only time in her career, and it reveals her teeth (courtesy of the Academy of Motion Picture Arts and Sciences).

Pola Negri in Ernst Lubitsch's silent *Passion*, which introduced both Negri and Emil Johnson to American audiences.

Others playing Du Barry roles include Norma Talmadge in *DuBarry, Woman of Passion* (1928), her last film, and Gladys George in M-G-M's *Marie Antoinette* (1938) with John Barrymore. Perhaps the most exquisite Du Barry of all was Dolores Del Rio, in the 1934 version of *Madame DuBarry*. Lucille

Ball was another Du Barry, starring with Red Skelton in Cole Porter's *DuBarry Was a Lady* (1943).

Films of 1918

Slowing down a bit, Bara appeared in only six movies in 1918. They were *The Forbidden Path, The Soul of Buddha, Under the Yoke, When a Woman Sins, Salome* and *The She-Devil.*

The Forbidden Path was a melodrama of artist life in Greenwich Village, scripted by E. Lloyd Sheldon from his own story. Theda played Nellie Lynn, who in her time poses as both the Madonna and — to get revenge against the man who wronged her — as "Sin." This movie was somewhat different from the typical Theda vampire plots, in that she was not intrinsically evil from the opening shot, though she made up for it at the end of the film. The other performers were Hugh Thompson, Sidney Mason, Walter Law, Florence Martin, Wynne H. Allen and Alphonse Ethier. In this "throbbing story of everyday life," the *Boston Post*'s reviewer found "a very trashy story."

The Soul of Buddha, from Theda Bara's own story, was a romantic tragedy about an alluring Javanese temple priestess who breaks her vows to woo and destroy her Scotsman lover and so meets with death at the hands of her high priest, who has pursued her to a Paris cafe where she dances. She was, she said, inspired by the 1917 execution of Mata Hari and by the Buddhist religion, which "in itself has the very undercurrent of mysticism that has appealed to all classes of men and women" (*Los Angeles Examiner*). Her costars were Hugh Thompson, Victor Kennard, Anthony Merlow, Florence Martin, Jack Ridgeway and Henry Warwick. Louella Parsons, never a friend, wrote that it was "difficult to take either Miss Bara or the play seriously. To see it is to laugh."

Under the Yoke was a melodrama of rebellion in the Philippines from a story by George Scarborough. Bara played Maria Valverde in what was advertised as "A Volcanic Drama of the Philippines — She Scorched Her Soul to Save an American Cavalry Officer." With her were Albert Roscoe, G. Raymond Nye, E. B. Tilton and Carrie Clark Ward.

Maria returns from the convent school to her father's estate and is sought in marriage by young Diablo Ramirez (Nye), a Filipino native. Her Spanish father has him thrown off the estate and Diablo swears revenge. Later, during a rebellion against the Americans, the father is killed by Diablo's band of rebels. When Diablo takes Maria's home — and Maria — a young American captain (Roscoe) comes to her rescue but is in turn captured. The captain and Maria escape, wire for reinforcements and in the ensuing battle the captain kills Diablo.

When a Woman Sins, a romantic melodrama based on a Betta Breuil story, had Theda as Lillian Marchand, a nurse who becomes Poppea, a heartless dancer

and idol of the libertines. Advertised as "The Greatest Woman's Story Ever Filmed — The Regeneration of a Modern Vampire," this film also starred Albert Roscoe, Joseph Swickard, Ogden Crane, Alfred Fremont and Jack Rollens.

Salome, a Biblical tragedy in which Theda played the young step-daughter of Herod who covets the head of John the Baptist, also starred Nye, Roscoe, Blinn, Fremont, Heyes, Bertram Grassby and Vera Doria.

In 1923 Nazimova made a very stylized version of the same story, and 30 years later Columbia released a talking version with Rita Hayworth doing the Dance of the Seven Veils.

Theda collapsed during the filming of this picture (whether "due to the strength of the California sun, or to the exotic warmth of the role she is now playing" the *San Francisco Chronicle* was unsure). But a complete recovery was apparently achieved, the film was concluded and she made a short return to New York. She would suffer fainting spells during a few more film productions.

In the Fox version, history as the Bible relates it is overthrown. Salome is not related to Herodias, her mother; rather, she plots to overthrow Herodias and the latter's brother so that she might seduce Herod. John the Baptist saves Herod and the royal entourage from a destructive natural force. Unlike the character in the Oscar Wilde play the Baptist is shown not as an older man but as a beardless and handsome youth. These departures disturbed some critics while Bara's costumes disturbed others. In St. Louis, as reported by the *Toledo Blade*, the costumes were censored as being "overbold and underclad, making too seductive an appeal to the senses." *Variety*, probably a little more artistic, opined that the "scarcity of her attire ... makes it most fascinating and devoid of vulgarity." However, the writer for *Theatre* magazine stated that "just how *Salome* is going to get by in cities where the Board of Censors is anything but a joke is beyond me." Theda replied to all of these that "if proper interpretation of the story calls for scantily-clad creatures the latter is only an incident. The body is beautiful — people make it 'imperfect' by contorting it with corsets [and] tight collars."

Of *Salome* the *New York Times* critic wrote, "For richness and extent of pageantry, sumptuousness of setting, and color details [it] has few equals among motion picture productions.... Theda Bara in the title role," it continued to her chagrin, "was all that those who have seen her in other films might expect — every minute the vampire."

"As Salome," she explained, "I tried to absorb the poetic impulses of Oscar Wilde. I tried to interpret the extraordinary, the hopeless moral

Opposite: **A still from *Salome* showing G. Raymond Nye as Herod (far left, foreground) and Albert Roscoe as John the Baptist between Nye and Bara (courtesy of the Academy of Motion Picture Arts and Sciences).**

disintegration of a woman's soul. The lines of Oscar Wilde's drama of *Salome*, are vivid paintings of human demoralization. Of course," she went on, lamenting, "I was again accused of emphasizing wickedness on the screen.... Other famous tragediennes have given us characterizations in the theatre of complex women and they have not been accused of being vampires. Why not I, Theda Bara?"

The She-Devil was a melodramatic romance of Paris and Old Spain, in which Theda played Lolette, belle of Juanquera. The script was by George Neje Hopkins, her close friend and dress designer (known familiarly as "Neje"). Advertised as "The Story of a Woman Who Raised Havoc with a Dozen Lovers," Theda played with Albert Roscoe, Frederick Bond and George McDaniel. By the time she made this movie one newspaper was calling her a star who "has grown in brilliancy until now she is probably the best known actress of the screen."

Lolette leaves her Spanish village to follow her current lover, an artist, to Paris. In a cafe she demonstrates how to properly dance the flamenco, and all of Paris' impresarios want to sign her up. She takes money from all of them but leaves it in the poor box at a church. Her artist lover convinces her to flee with him, since she will be wanted by the police for fraud. Meanwhile, an old lover, a bandit from her village, has found her in Paris and continues to pursue her and the artist in their escape. She tricks the bandit into letting them escape, in what *Variety* called "an elaborate and atmospheric" film.

Films of 1919

In 1919 Theda Bara made seven movies for Fox. They were *The Light*, *When Men Desire*, *The Siren's Song*, *A Woman There Was*, *Kathleen Mavourneen*, *La Belle Russe* and *The Lure of Ambition*. Compared with her earlier vamp films, these were commercial flops. Theda and Mary Pickford had both attained success in their type roles. The public would not accept a mature Pickford, nor would it accept a non-vamp Theda Bara.

The Light was a romantic drama of regeneration, filmed in New Orleans, in which Theda played Blanchette Dumond, a.k.a. Madame Lefresne, from a story by Luther Reed and Brett Page. The other actors were Eugene Ormande, Robert Walker, George Renevant and Florence Martin. *Variety*'s opinion was that it was "a fairly good type of Bara production."

It is the story of a woman of loose morals rejected for Red Cross work in wartime Paris. Since she cannot even help the dying, she decides to dance for the dead. A young sculptor sees her dancing in the graveyard and wants her to pose for him. The sculptor is eventually sent to the war and is blinded. Discharged from the army, he is cared for by Blanchette. While Blanch64

A studio publicity shot showing Theda's long hair to its best advantage (courtesy of the Academy of Motion Picture Arts and Sciences).

ette is fulfilling her nursing ambitions one of her old lovers comes back and angrily taunts the two of them. The sculptor replies that as a blind man he can see the beauty of her soul, something which the sighted ex-lover obviously cannot.

When Men Desire, a World War I spy movie in which Bara played Marie Lohr, was from a story by E. L. Sheldon and J. S. Dawley. It was advertised as "Woman Outraged — the Thrilling Adventures of a Woman Who Tried to Be True." Bara's costars were Flemming Ward, G. Raymond Nye, Edward Eikas, Florence Martin and Maude Hill.

The Siren's Song was a romantic melodrama in which Theda played Marie Bernais, a Breton peasant daughter of a lighthouse keeper who becomes a great diva. The other performers were Alfred Fremont, Ruth Handforth, L. C. Shumway, Albert Roscoe, Paul Weigel and Carrie Clark Ward.

A Woman There Was, scripted from a story by Neje, was a romantic drama of the South Seas in which Theda played the Princess Zara. It was the last Bara movie directed by J. Gordon Edwards or scripted by Adrian Johnson. Her costars were William (or Winthrop) Davidson (1888–1947), Robert Elliott, Claude Payton and John Ardizoni.

Zara's father rules over a pearl-fishing kingdom to which a young American missionary comes. The wild Zara decides to marry him, an idea which appeals neither to her intended nor to her savage lovers. There are some natural disasters and she is stabbed by mistake, thus resolving the missionary's problem. It was a very disjointed production which *Variety* felt "will offend no one [though] it is stupid and unattractive."

By this time Bara was growing weary and admitting that she did not think much of the movies she had made. "When transported to the movies," she cried, "magnificent tragedies, such as *La giaconda*, become painfully inarticulate attempts." But, she praised her cameramen. "My cameraman is my artistic speedometer. If he likes a scene, I know it's good; if he shakes his head I sometimes cry a little because I am so tired, but I always do a re-take." Many may find it difficult to work up a great deal of sympathy for her well-compensated tiredness when so many in her time worked endless hours for scant reward.

Kathleen Mavourneen, a romance of Old Ireland in which Theda played an Irish peasant girl, Kathleen Cavanagh, was directed and scripted by Charles Brabin (the mere sight of whom fascinated her) from a poem by Tom Moore and a play by Dion Boucicault. Advertised as "The Sweetest Irish Love Story Ever Told," it also featured Edward O'Connor, Jennie Dickerson, Raymond McKee, Marc McDermott, Marcia Harris, Henry Hallam, Harry Gripp and Morgan Thorpe. Theda asked for the title role and Fox gave it to her in hopes of boosting her sagging popularity.

It had the opposite effect. Hibernian societies caused chaos at many theaters because an Irish heroine was being played by a Jewish actress. At the Sun, in San Francisco, a mob of young Irishmen, angry at the depiction of pigs in an Irish parlor and inflamed by two Catholic priests, rioted and caused $3,000 damage to the theater and its projection equipment.

Not everyone of Irish heritage reacted that way. Bara's mailman gave her a green shawl which had been his "sainted mother's." He believed, the *Cleveland News* reported, that his "mother would rather have an Irish colleen [sic] wearing it than the moths eating it."

Variety reviewed the film as

> a dramatization of the old Irish song, in which Theda Bara does her best to dissociate herself from "vampire" parts. Her trouble, however, is that she has to make the effort. She is forever acting, posing with an exaggerated air of sweetness, shedding in every direction the light of her smiles. Her director, nevertheless has gotten some good local color into his arrangements. The lighting effects, too, are excellent and almost as good as in "Evangeline," and when you have said that you've said something.
>
> Kathleen is an Irish colleen. Seeing her at Donnybrook Fair, the Squire falls in love with her and sends his agent to her father and mother to tell them that they must pay or be evicted. To pay is beyond them. As the price of

letting them alone he tells Kathleen that he will accept her in marriage. Desperate, she takes him, but her own true love, meanwhile, has been busy in an effort to save her. So, by the usual route, the story works through the accepted dramatic conclusion.

La Belle Russe was a romantic melodrama set in Paris and London. Theda played a dual role as twin sisters, the virtuous Fleurette Sackton, and the notorious "La Belle Russe," who poses as the virtuous twin. Directed and scripted by Brabin, the story came from a play by David Belasco. The other stars were Warburton Gamble, Marian Stewart, Robert Lee Keeling, William Davidson, Alice Wilson and Robert Vivian.

The Lure of Ambition, Bara's last Fox film, was a romantic melodrama based on a Julia Burnham story and directed by Edmund Lawrence. Bara played Olga Dolan with costars Thurlow Bergen, William Davidson, Dan Mason, Ida Waterman, Amelia Gardner, Robert P. Gibbs, Dorothy Drake, Peggy Parr and Tammany Young.

SIX.
The Reel Vampire,
the Real Theda

*T*he outbreak of World War I brought many changes to American life and the national outlook, including a new self-confidence and materialism. Mary Pickford (1893–1979) and the Griffith girls (one of whom was Lillian Gish, 1896-1993) had conformed to the Pollyanna ideals of the prewar world but in their screen roles, in 1915 Theda Bara brought a different idol, the glowering *femme fatale.* "With her robust voluptuousness, her relentless eyes and her encircling arms, [she] was the accepted prototype of the lady who made men uneasy, from St. Anthony to Rudyard Kipling," according to a 1927 reviewer who probably was already aware that her films had established sex as the *sine qua non* of American films, with domestic intrigue, marital infidelity and the triangle drama as dominant motifs.

She started a fad. Her example was followed by whole harems of women-of-the-world heroines, for whom (a 1936 article recalled) "she set the pace." The vamp role seemed created for Theda. But there were other vamp-like actresses seeking to cash in on her success.

There had been other *femmes fatales* before Theda: Olga Nethersole, famed for her Soul Kiss, made male heart beats quicken in 1900; Kitty Gordon made backs famous in 1906; and such figures as Lina Cavalieri in 1908, Mary Garden (who played Salome in 1909), Pauline Frederick in 1910 and the musical Valeska Suratt in 1912 all inflamed the passions of male fans. But Theda Bara was the queen before whom these others paled. As for the Griffith stars (the Gish sisters, Blanche Sweet, Bessie Love *et al.*) who radiated Victorian ideals of sweet innocence, they too were in eclipse. Both types depended on unsophisticated audiences with the narrowest experiences of life — rustics, the urban poor and the young.

Theda Bara's phenomenal success unleashed an army of now-forgotten competitors, and for half a decade the movies were overrun with female wickedness. Among her imitators were Francesca Bertini, Lyda Borelli and

La Hesperia, all of whom had reigned in Italy, hanging from velvet curtains while their male supplicants sipped champagne from their poisoned slippers. Pola Negri (1899-1987), according to *Glamour Girls* authors Parish and Stanke, was the transatlantic link that imported these dark foreboding females to sunny California to seek their fortune, but to no avail.

Half-woman, half-demon, they had but to crook a finger and any man would leave family, home and job eagerly to become putty in their hands. They took money from their victims — not as whores, to spend it on luxuries or put in the bank, but merely to ruin their victims. Such unbelievable behavior became ridiculous in some cases where the vamp in question was not particularly beautiful, sensual or alluring.

Theda Bara already was vamping her way to a scandalous American triumph before Pola Negri made her celluloid debut. But strangely Charles Ford, in his *La Vie Quotidienne à Hollywood*, makes no mention of the immortal Theda while discussing the role of the vamp as a leading female character of the early movies.

The other American actresses Frank Powell had considered and rejected for *A Fool There Was* — Valeska Suratt and Virginia Pearson — were both signed by Fox as second-string vamps. Louise Glaum, Dorothy Dalton, Olga Petrova and many another talented actress leapt into the limelight at other studios as hell-bent vamps, and even established artists like Clara Kimball Young (1890-1960) (in *Lola*) and Anita Stewart (1896-1961) (in *The Yellow Typhoon*) took at least one fling at vamping. The glamour of the "copycat" vampire ladies was closely associated with evil, and their sensuality was suffused in the aura of imminent peril of the black widow spider.

With these new women came new heroes, more debonair than the solid, almost middle-aged leading men of prewar films. The English language, meanwhile, not only incorporated the word "vampire" but its derivatives "vamp" and "baby vamp" (an early expression for what would later be called the "teeny bopper"), while the sublime subtitle "Kiss me, my fool" was quoted for a couple of generations before ending up as "Kiss me, *you* fool" from the loud mouth of Joanne Worley on Rowan and Martin's *Laugh-In* in the late 1960s.

The vampire tradition that went back to the nineteenth century was rooted in a fascination with sinful love, salvation, and a fear of God, flesh and the devil. The Fox-Bara addition was the modern notion of sex appeal — with, as Alex Walker noted, the emphasis on "appeal" as something positive and pleasurable, at least until the final reckoning. The morality of the pre–1914 dramas preached many of the homely virtues of the working classes; the trend that Theda Bara and her imitators set, somewhat crudely, was to make screen sex fascinating to the growing middle-class audiences. She was immediately successful because she was exactly the kind of sex symbol Americans wanted at the time. Her appearance and her femininity were so exaggerated and her movie plots so outlandish that she really presented no threat to conventional morality and the average woman. In a curious way, Lockwood felt that she even reinforced the remnants of strict Victorian convention by humiliating and destroying the men who gave in to their baser passions for her. All of this Fox exploited.

Fox was not the first to exploit sex in cinema. In 1913 Carl Laemmle's studio produced — without his foreknowledge — *Traffic in Souls*, a film about the white slave trade, which made Laemmle's Independent Motion Picture studio a profit of 770 percent.

Unlike earlier, apparently shrill-voiced vampires, Theda's vampire had a voice as sweet and soothing as the sound of harp strings. Yet, in those silent film days, who would know or care? Still, it was "not the voice," wrote movie columnist Archie Bell in 1915, "of the usual and traditional vampire woman on the stage." This may or may not have pleased Fox, Selig and Goldfarb. What followed in the column must have, however: "The artists and specialists in crime have called her face the most cruel and wicked in the world. Bernard Shaw's specialist in 'Pygmalion' would find the coils of the python or ancient oriental poison in her voice." A campaign to prove her evil without peer was launched in the wake of *A Fool There Was.* Heyes, whose father Herbert had starred often with Bara, recalled that for the campaign "Fox unleashed an avalanche of stills showing the beauty-that-drove-men-mad in bare-shouldered frolics with serpents (of the Nile), bats (vampire), mummies (Egyptian), ravens (black), skulls and skeletons (human, male) and other things nice girls don't mess around with."

Her face, which was intense and sensual with heavy-lidded eyes, became famous everywhere, as did the props — her symbols of evil — that were always photographed with her. She was described (and accepted) as having the "wickedest face in the world, dark-brooding, beautiful and heartless"; she was draped in dark silks with her white shoulders and arms bare, and in contrast to the prim, innocent prewar cinema heroines, she was the quintessential voluptuary who required love and riches and stopped at nothing to attain them. For the World War I generation this was as daring as possible.

Forty years later, her obituary in the *New York Times* recalled "the ageless siren, luring men into tragedy with rolling eyes, heavy make-up and scanty costumes" while the *Los Angeles Times* credited her "heavy-lidded beauty" with the luring of "customers to the box offices by the thousands."

What had they come to see? Until the use of the word "vamp" there was no convenient phrase in use to describe her character or what she did, exactly. Heyes recalled that this deadly, lustful, lascivious, carnal, heartless, soulless she-demon "like the succubus of yore [would] drain the manhood out of men. She'd cast them aside like empty peanut shells, and (just to be mean) she'd grind them under her high spiked heels." Not only were they not

Two very different bird poses. *Above:* With her left wrist cradling the neck of a faintly visible raven in a shot labeled "Theda Bara, 1918, Cinematic Queen of Sin" (courtesy UCLA Arts Library, Special Collections).

Opposite: A much softer image, with baby chicks — more the real Theda than her usual portrayal (courtesy of the Academy of Motion Picture Arts and Sciences).

disappointed, they apparently loved it for her role made Fox a viable, profitable studio.

Fox's publicity department assured all who cared that the screen portrayal of the vampire was not intended to condone its evilness, but rather to point out that evil consumes itself. Victor Freeburg, a professor at Columbia University, opined to Roberta Courtlandt of *Motion Picture* about Theda's "potent influence for good." "Most girls are good," he asserted, "but good girls do not want to see other good girls on the screen. There's no interest, no fascination, in that for them. This is another reason for Miss Bara's success; she shows them something vastly different from the life they know. Few are either daring enough or desirous enough of leading a vampire existence, but through the medium of Theda Bara they can do her deeds and live her life. Their emotions are enriched by just that much."

For her part Theda told Mary Mullett of *American Magazine* that she was the "embodiment of a secret dream which all of us have or have had." Asking if any woman had not dreamed of being loved by a man so completely that he would "count the world well lost if he could gain the prize of her love," she flashed her vamp eyes and answered her own question. "It is a craving to love and be loved without counting the cost... a desire to be beautifully wicked" that made the vampire attractive to film audiences.

Those vamp eyes and sneer had become her trademark, but were the looks she cast from the rolling eyes genuine? Probably not, according to an interesting tale from Nita Naldi (1898–1961). In 1955 Naldi, speaking of the passionate and evil sirens of those early films, told Ezra Goodman, "We were all blind as bats. Theda Bara couldn't see a foot ahead of her and poor Rudy [Valentino] groped his way through many a love scene and I really mean groped. They all used big reflectors to get extra light from the sun — that's how we acquired that interesting Oriental look." And Miriam Cooper, never passing up a chance to take a cat swipe at Theda, remarked that the latter's *was* a searching look. "She was so nearsighted she had to look hard to see anything a foot in front of her nose. She couldn't even see the camera. She kept walking into it and knocking it over." Her goddaughter, June Millarde Stanley, said that "Aunt Theda was blind as a bat" due to an unspecified childhood problem.

Her dentist in later life, Dr. Edward Furstman of West Los Angeles, recalled that whenever he was in her house it was quite dark. She and her husband had problems with cataracts and their eyes were sensitive to light. At that time, the late 1940s and early 1950s, her husband never let her go anywhere by herself. Her poor vision was probably the reason for the precaution.

As to her physical appearance Theda once asserted that brunettes were actually less calculating and cold-blooded than blondes, but added that as a vampire she had to be a brunette "because the popular idea of a wicked woman is a dark and midnight beauty." At the same time she was unimpressed by the amount of dramatic talent required for her parts since, she observed, "a rolling eye and an undraped figure was all that the public required of a vampire."

Her sister disliked the vamp movies, telling anyone who would listen in later years that Theda was nothing like that. The resentment was such that, while she displayed some Theda pictures, nothing remotely vampish ever appeared on her walls.

At the time, however, Theda went along with all of the image-building. Though she later admitted that the idea of playing a vampire appealed not at all (and that eventually "the word vampire became a stench in my cinematograph nostrils"), she stated in 1915, after filming exteriors for *The Devil's Daughter*, that the vampire type of woman appealed to her artistic sense: "There are such women, plenty of them. I have made an especial study of the type. It is a highly interesting one. I am delighted to have this opportunity of displaying my work to American spectators and I hope I have succeeded in depicting the complex emotions of the panther woman as vividly as they have appealed to me."

Showing the genuine closeness between Theda (seated) and her sister, Lori (courtesy of the Academy of Motion Picture Arts and Sciences).

During the height of her popularity, Bara once announced with a straight face that her greatest inspirations for playing the vamp roles came to her while she was enjoying a good hot bath. At the same time she cultivated the personality that had been created for her. She accentuated her eyes with dark shadow and mascara, the stereotypical look of the sinful woman, and wore indigo costumes to accentuate her ghostly whiteness. After moving to Los Angeles she filled her large pseudo–Tudor house on West Adams (after a short stay at an impressive looking house at 2285 La Granada in Hollywood) with such mysteriously sensual things as tiger-skin rugs, crystal balls and skulls while she practiced her two favorite hobbies, astrology and perfume distillation.

The latter interest was sparked when Al Selig dropped mention of a "psychic perfume" especially designed to publicize Theda's role in *Cleopatra*. He got her excited about the idea and, as the *Film Daily* recalled in 1931, she took up the "study of perfumes in a Serious Way…. She spent several thousands in research experts to discover the types of perfume Cleopatra used and had these all blended into one."

It must be remembered when considering all of this Bara-vamp legend

Theda lounges in a swing at her West Adams home (courtesy of the Academy of Motion Picture Arts and Sciences).

that the injection of her vampire role into a carefully thought-out private life was only one instance of Hollywood's growing dependence on public relations hype in early film days. Little was known of the stars' private lives before the gossip columnists and movie magazines sprang forth, so audiences thought that if an actress played a glamorous role she obviously lived that way at home. In point of fact, in the 1910s most actors and actresses lived in hotel rooms or modest apartments, and drove their own cars, if they even owned such, to the studio. Lillian Gish, who came to Hollywood to play in *Birth of a Nation*, rode the streetcar. Mary Pickford was hardly the innocent pre-pubescent she portrayed.

In 1913 Florence Lawrence (1886-1938) became the first film actress to be identified by name. Film producers were reluctant to risk paying higher salaries to actors who had been given billing, but the public, ripe for fantastic film star images, reassured them that such higher salaries would result in box office profits in the stratosphere. Thus was born the star system.

Film historian Richard deCordova, examining the origins of the star system and trying to untangle the web between the truth and the press agents' copy, put its development in four distinct stages. The notion that people act

An autographed photo showing the exotic look that Fox cultivated (courtesy of the Academy of Motion Picture Arts and Sciences).

in films emerged in a 1907 discourse on acting. The picture personality appeared in 1909 as actors were first described as an "image" or a "personality" as a result of their multiple appearances in films. Then, around 1913, the private lives of the actors became the principal focus of articles. In the early twenties the morality of the stars' private lives was called into question and publicity began to focus on the unconventional and scandalous aspects of their lives. This, deCordova asserts, brought about the Hays Office and censorship.

How did agents in that third stage of deCordova's division (1913-1920) handle the private lives of other stars? To foster Mary Pickford's image as "America's Sweetheart," her studio distributed countless photos showing her dressed as a young girl, playing with puppies, kittens and even bunnies. Actually, she was a thrice-married homewrecker. Essanay Studios shamelessly reported that their romantic idol Francis X. Bushman (1883-1966), who actually had a wife and five children, was single and available to any woman who could catch him. Thousands of American females believed this, and Essanay had to hire eight secretaries just to answer "King Romeo's" fan mail and three stockboys to carry the autographed pictures to the post office. Other studios followed this example with any "discoveries" they had made.

The public took to Theda immediately, and an unknown became world famous in less than a year because of her vamp role in *A Fool There Was*. Her film career fit neatly into deCordova's third stage and what followed in her career helps to prove his thesis. Unsophisticated movie audiences tended to believe what they saw on the screen. But, at the same time, the public — as P. T. Barnum was fond of saying — liked to be humbugged. Movie historian Charles Lockwood asserts, "Even many of the fans who doubted the stories about Theda Bara's exotic origins or her ability to make men grovel at her feet wanted to believe that all this was true…. Because most fans had not learned that [movie acting was not reality] the studios and the stars encouraged these illusions to sell more tickets."

Along these same lines, historian Benjamin Hampton observed, "movie stars were accepted into the public's affections to an extent unknown to stage players." The principal stage players of the day continued to be known to their ardent admirers as *Mr.* Southern, *Miss* Adams, *Miss* Fiske. But almost at once movie fans began to talk about "Mary" (Mary Pickford), "Bunny" (John Bunny), "Broncho Billy" (G. M. Anderson), "Tom" (Tom Mix) and "Theda." The instantaneous spread of star interest surprised the entire industry.

SEVEN.

The Vampire:
Desired and Despised

*B*y February 1916 the *New York Times* estimated (by calculating the number of film prints, theaters, seats and daily performances) that half a million people a day — or 182 million a year — were seeing Theda Bara, "the Flaming Comet of the Cinema Firmament." Not all were admirers. In 1915 Bara told Archie Bell that "A woman walked into a New York theater and kicked a hole in my face on a poster in the lobby." No less a figure than President Woodrow Wilson, reflecting the stern morals of his Scots Presbyterian upbringing, disliked the films of Bara and her imitators, preferring (especially when he was deathly ill in 1919-20) outdoor films with horses, cowboys, Western deserts and mountains.

A critic of somewhat lesser stature was Gilbert Seldes (1893–1970), who criticized sex-appeal movies in a 1929 article for *Century Magazine*, endorsing censorship and happily asserting that those movies (especially Theda's) were forgettable and forgotten. In this he reflected *New York Times* critic Alexander Woolcott's opinion that Theda's performances were not so bad as to be unforgettable. Apparently neither gentleman had read Marion Brooks Ritchie's 1928 interview of Theda in *Screenland*, in which she assured the interviewee that "there are loads and loads of us in every land" who still cared about her and were curious about her happiness. In the Bell interview Bara said, "The other day on my way to the studio, I saw a group of children standing gazing at a cart of fruit. I went up, bought them a fine basket of fruit and gave it to them. They were delighted until one little girl screeched out: 'It's the vampire woman.' Their smiles turned to expressions of fright and they dropped the fruit as if it were poison. I called them to me and talked with them; and finally, we became friends."

Along the same lines, an oft-repeated anecdote tells of a mother who saw her child walking along a quiet New York street talking to a dark, white-faced lady . On recognizing Theda, the mother began to shriek wildly, "Save him, save him, the vampire has my child!" and actually called the police.

Children were not overly fond of this scary lady, though if they actually met her they found her to be warm and kind. A woman in Piedmont, California, named Virginia Leach fondly recalls that the actress played with her when she was a two-year-old visiting Palm Springs at the turn of the 1920s. More typical was theatrical agent Alan Brock, who recalled that "all of us kids avoided movie vampires, only being held captive when their pictures were forced upon us by the lure of a Pearl White serial. Pearl was our type of heroine — the gal who socked the bad guy! Miss Bara sipping champagne from a thin-stemmed crystal as she mesmerized the hero only made us squirm."

On the other hand, famed writer S. J. Perelman in 1952 recalled that, as a sixth grade schoolboy in 1914-15, he was once condemned to stay after school for fighting with a bully. While cleaning erasers, he "accidentally got my first intimation of Miss Bara from a couple of teachers excitedly discussing her." He recalled the conversation as follows:

> "If you rearrange the letters in her name, they spell 'Arab Death,'" one of them was saying, with a delicious shudder. "I've never seen an actress kiss the way she does. She just sort of glues herself onto a man and drains the strength out of him."
>
> "I know — isn't it revolting?" sighed the other rapturously. "Let's go see her again tonight!" Needless to add, I was in the theatre before either of them, and my reaction was no less fervent. For a full month afterward, I gave myself up to fantasies in which I lay with my head pillowed in the seductress's lap, intoxicated by coal-black eyes smoldering with belladonna. At her bidding, I eschewed family, social position, my brilliant career — a rather hazy combination of African explorer and private sleuth — to follow her to the ends of the earth. I saw myself, oblivious to everything but the nectar of her lips, being cashiered for cheating at cards (I was also a major in the Horse Dragoons), descending to drugs, and ultimately winding up as a beach-comber in the South Seas, with a saintly, ascetic face like H. B. Warner's.

Because of her roles and scant costumes, Bara was denounced by the clergy. The Kansas Board of Censors perpetually went gunning for her films, too; in fact it rejected the first four in toto. In those days before the Hays Office was created to unify and coordinate film censorship in 1921, each state or locality had its own censorship board. Historian George Pratt notes that the dour Kansans, besides the four rejections, chopped up *Gold and the Woman* by ordering the elimination of two murder scenes, all love scenes between the guardian and the vampire and all cigarette scenes, as well as the shortening of the drinking scenes to a flash. They also slashed *Cleopatra*, ordering the elimination of Cleopatra's "suggestive advances" on Caesar, the closeups of Cleopatra's embraces with Caesar and Antony, and all closeups of exposed limbs, breasts and abdomen. One suspects that the censors had not been awake in their ancient history class, for how would they have explained Caesar's subsequent Egyptian involvement had it not been for Cleopatra's "suggestive advances"? But the censor's fearful mind is rarely bothered by veracity, historical or contemporary.

They next attacked *When Men Desire*, ordering the elimination of certain titles such as "Like a fool, I thought I'd have to marry you to possess you." In *The She-Devil* a scene showing a girl smoking was eliminated. In *Salome* they ordered the elimination of Salome's bathing scene at the beginning, the shortening of Salome's visit to John the Baptist's cell, and the elimination of Salome lying beside John the Baptist's head on a platter. They may have been distraught at not being able to cut the biblically sound reason for Herod's rash oath upon seeing Salome's dance.

Taking a peek at censorship one sees several ironic twists. As Hollywood broadened its appeal, it came under closer scrutiny from church and women's groups, a press that had formerly been ga-ga, and outsiders who resented its affluent hedonism. Raoul Walsh recalled that "every state had its own censors and Pennsylvania was the toughest. Whenever anybody took a scene that was the least bit off, everybody would yell: 'It won't be shown in Pennsylvania!' But we battled on. Sometimes we'd take maybe six or seven risque scenes, hoping they'd leave two."

A wave of scandals in the early twenties including the Fatty Arbuckle murder trial, Wallace Reid's death and the William Desmond Taylor murder led the Hollywood magnates to toss their problems in the lap of Will H. Hays, a devout Presbyterian who left President Warren Harding's cabinet to become czar of the movies' public relations. As official moral guardian, Hays served zealously for 23 years.

According to some, Hays bade the tide of censorship to recede and it did. This achievement, according to those same supporters, was due to his introduction of a "voluntary" code of "don'ts" and "be carefuls." In reality, all that Hays accomplished was to replace the local censor boards that dotted the nation with a centralized one, the National Board of Review. The effect was to stifle American creativity.

The Production Code which the Hays Office issued consisted of 50 applications, including the following examples:

> I.1.a. The technique of murder must be presented in a way that will not inspire imitation.
>
> I.3. Illegal drug traffic must never be presented.
>
> I.4. The use of liquor in American life, when not required by the plot or for the proper characterization, will not be shown.
>
> II.2.c. In general, passion should be so treated that these scenes do not stimulate the lower and baser element.
>
> II.6. Miscegenation (sex relationships between white and black races) is forbidden.

"Knockout drops for eyes": a lovely shot on the front porch of her home (courtesy UCLA Arts Library, Special Collections).

II.8. Scenes of actual child birth, in fact or in silhouette, are never to be presented.
VI.4. Dancing costumes intended to permit undue exposure or indecent movements in the dance are forbidden.

Gene Fowler, writing in the *Hollywood Reporter* in 1934, began an attack on the "wit-nit babblings, stale violet fancies and imbecile-antics of censors" which culminated in his "Ten Commandments for the Motion Picture Industry" in 1936. Four of them follow:

1st. Thou shall not photograph a lady and gentleman in bed together, even though said lady and gentleman have been properly introduced, one to the other. Thou mayst try it but thou wilt get thyself into one hell of a jam. In the wicked city of Chicago, minions of the law did break in and find one buckaroo in such aforesaid state with two ladies of blonde extraction and he did cry out that he learned such trick from the movies. To wit that such scenes are hereby decreed subversive of the public morals.

3rd. Thou shalt not photograph the wiggling belly, the gleaming thigh or the winking navel, especially to music, as goings-on of this ilk sorely troubleth the little boys of our land and so crammeth the theatres with adolescence that papa cannot find a seat.

8th. If thou givest thy audience a stick-up, thou'll be damn careful, for thou art giving idea to the immature dope, with which our fair land aboundeth in plenty, and thou'll find thyself up the creek in New York and Pennsylvania — places of money.

9th. Thou shalt not give tongue to vulgar expressions, to wit, "Nuts," for such invective hath a peculiar significance to the spinsters of this world and is held by them as having biological import.

As usual, where Theda was concerned, the censors were out of touch with the majority: hundreds were turned away on the opening night of *Cleopatra*, in which, a 1936 newspaper writer recalled, "she wore no more clothing than was deemed necessary at that time. Her audiences were enjoying themselves hugely."

The vamp lady did have an admiring following. In the Bell interview she revealed that she got "letters from Egypt, Syria, China, Australia, South America … in fact from all over the world," and Al Selig reportedly told a film columnist in 1931 about "one Rajah of India [who] sent her over a period of a year precious jewels, gorgeous tapestries, shawls, embroideries." Her humble admirers, too, "in odd corners of the earth, forwarded little inexpensive mementos that they had treasured for years."

She kept all the fan mail she received and reportedly enjoyed reading her "billets-doux." One fan wrote: "It is over a month since you last heard from me…. It has required all my will-power to keep from writing you unduly." Another expressed a more elaborate left-handed devotion: "Theda Bara, the Xantippe of the screen, the living Jezebel of the present-age. To this genius of her kind, endowed with a weird beauty … Does not the film loving world owe to this far-from-vapid actress a debt of gratitude for her faithful portrayal of her age-old predecessors so famous now both in allegory and reality?"

Other fans concentrated on her eyes, one describing her as "the lady with knockout drops for eyes," while Martha McKelvie in *Motion Picture* concluded that those eyes were due to nearsightedness. Theda replied in another magazine, *Motion Picture Classic*, that it was "rather mean" to say that. According to Gayla Jamison Hamilton another fan found more than her eyes to celebrate with a little rhyme:

> Those eyes, those lips,
> That hair, those earrings!
> Make all the menfolks
> Lose their bearings!

But some critics, notably a writer in the *Montgomery Journal*, found something to criticize: "Although Mlle. Bara is a wonderfully beautiful woman, she has cultivated a sinister droop to her left eye and a cruel expression of the mouth, which help much in her portrayal of the wickedest women ever written about."

Like the children with the fruit cart, others altered their opinions. The woman who kicked in the poster in a theater lobby in 1915 later wrote to Theda about the incident and apologized. As Theda saw it, "They hate me, and then their hate turns to pity, and pity is akin to love." Actually, despite the fearful mother and the kicking woman, Theda Bara seems to have appealed more to women than to men because, as she observed, "the vampire I play is the vengeance of my sex upon its exploiters. I have the face of a vampire, but the heart of a feminist."

The unwitting inciter of riots in a publicity photograph by Maurice Goldberg (courtesy of the Academy of Motion Picture Arts and Sciences).

Offscreen, of course, she was not a vampire, and she was careful to say so. She could not entirely discount the notion, however, or the public would question the authenticity of the screen roles. Still, the righteous matrons who patronized the vamp films would have been put off if she had truly been known as a vampire. To them, apparently, screen vampirism translated into their subconsciously evolving feminism.

For that matter Heyes recalls that after Theda played in *The Darling of Paris,* her feminist friends demanded that "she stick to sticking it to the men." As to her popularity with her own sex, the head of a New York department store pleaded with her, "Please don't come in, Miss Bara. We'll send the gowns to your hotel, but we can't stand any more of these riots." Just the day before, Bara had gone into the department store and touched one of the hats on display. After she left mobs of women had broken plate-glass windows and strewn merchandise all over the floor in a surge to grab the hat she had touched, in the hope that they might acquire some of Theda's power to make men grovel.

As Gayla Jamison Hamilton asks in her master's thesis on Bara and the vamp phenomenon, "Did a Mary Pickford film ever provoke a riot?" Theda's films caused at least three riots, in Boston, Cleveland and San Francisco. How many stores were the centers of the riots? No one knows. But aside from the angry Irishmen in San Francisco, her films infuriated the clergy of her native Cincinnati, including evangelist Billy Sunday, who protested against her costumes and film behavior.

To defend herself Theda wrote an open letter to the mayor of Cincinnati which appeared in *Motion Picture* in August 1917. "I have," she asserted, "just as definite a place, just as high a mission in pictures as the best of your evangelists and the most beloved of your local ministers. Through the silent but expressive medium of the motion picture I am saving hundreds of girls from social degradation and wrong-doing.... Furthermore, I am reaching one million persons each day — an audience larger than was ever had before by any man or woman in the world's history."

Other public encounters were pleasant. One fan, quoted in the *Detroit New Tribune,* wrote to tell her that he was having a house built in Marietta, Ohio, and was reserving a suite of rooms for her. The suite would not be used until she visited and would not be used again when she left. Another Ohioan, a strange Cincinnati man, was quoted in the *New York Telegraph* as requesting "one of your photographs to add to my collection. If any charges I will pay them. I think you are one of the most charming, artistic, good-looking actresses of the illegitimate [*sic*] stage."

At Christmas 1918 Theda Bara received two carloads of gifts from fans, including lingerie, a poodle, portraits of the vamp and an engraved German helmet from a soldier who had fought on the Western Front.

There was no question about the men liking her. During World War I the 58th Infantry adopted her as their godmother and presented her with a golden horseshoe. At the same time she, with many other actors and actresses, threw herself into the Liberty Loan War Bond drives.

EIGHT.

The Vamp's Influence
Sells War Bonds and Sex

*D*uring the last week of April 1918, a year after the United States became involved in World War I and after Theda Bara completed *When a Woman Sins*, there was a massive war-bond rally in Los Angeles' Central Park (now Pershing Square). The exigencies of the war forced Fox to let his vamp star come down to earth. The 1916 contract had barred her from appearing in public unveiled and in non-vamp dress. The war changed this. Each studio (Metro, Triangle, Fox and the rest) had separate nights when their stars would rouse the crowds to buy bonds.

Each star had a quota, depending on his or her popularity. Theda's quota was $50,000 for her night, Wednesday the 26th. She broke it by selling $56,950 worth, which the *Los Angeles Times* called "the greatest individual triumph," helping to put Southern California "over the top." As the *Times* reporter recounted it:

Miss Bara faced what was probably the largest audience that ever saw her in real life on the Pacific Coast. Within 30 minutes after she undertook the drive she was [moving] along at breakneck speed with all motion picture records in bond selling here shattered to smithereens.

Starting the drive by announcing that she would give $5,000 if 100 men in the audience would each take a $50 bond, she came dangerously near causing a riot. There were at least 15,000 people in the park and in the streets.... At the outset Miss Bara stated that she would autograph every Liberty Bond receipt that was handed up to her.

"Make me work hard!" she cried, and the crowd took her at her word. She wore out no less than a half a dozen good fountain pens, but at the finish she had neither writers' cramp nor lack of enthusiasm....

Miss Bara's campaign opened with a subscription for two $100 bonds by W. H. Taylor, aged 99.... It has been estimated that between 25,000 and 30,000 people visited Central Park some time during the afternoon.... [She] arrived in company with her sister, Loro [*sic*] Bara. Both were dressed in white suits.

71

Bara selling Liberty Bonds to eager buyers, showing a rarely photographed open-mouth smile (courtesy of the Academy of Motion Picture Arts and Sciences).

Theda Bara wore a dainty little pink sports hat. She made her bow to Los Angeles bond buyers as a public speaker of marked ability. She is a clear thinker, with a well-modulated voice and a delightful personality.

Her remarks could be heard distinctly across Central Park. "We are not assembled here today for the purpose of talking," she began. "We came here to buy and sell Liberty Bonds. This is Liberty Day and I wish that all of you could realize, as I do, that there is something of intense earnestness in the word 'Liberty.' It is more than the hollow sound of words, for it means that if you do not untie your purse strings and invest your money in Liberty Bonds the liberty that we have known so long is going to perish from the earth. When the war is over and we sit down to think the thing over dispassionately the question we will have to ask ourselves is this: 'When my country needed me what kind of service did I render unto her?'"

Today it is our privilege to loan our government the money to free this world from despotism forever and ever. When it is all over no slacker can rest in peace unless he has served his country in some important capacity. You can all buy Liberty Bonds. You must give and give and give for the sake of Old Glory.

When I was in New York during the second Liberty Loan drive I sold $300,000 worth of bonds, and I thought that was the happiest experience of my life. Come on friends, make this another red-letter day in the life of Theda Bara. Give and give and give and give for the sake of Our Country!

The Kaiser did not threaten the American way of life, but neither Bara nor her audience realized that. The crowd apparently wanted to do what they could to make it another red-letter day for Theda. In a time more nationalistic than our own it was possible to recount, as the reporter did, the story of one old newspaper woman who made her way to Theda and laid down $50 "which she said she had saved by the strictest economy for the purpose of equipping herself with a satisfactory set of teeth. She said she was willing to go without the teeth to win the war."

During the war Theda's brother (also a Fox employee, as assistant director to Kenean Buel, the director of "Baby Grands" Jane and Katherine Lee), served with the Signal Corps' aviation branch.

After the war Theda made the news again by being one of the first to buy the government's $1,000 Treasury Savings Certificate in July 1919. Comparing them to the War Savings Stamps and noting that they paid 4 percent interest compounded quarterly, she announced that "my investment of $836 in a certificate this month will result in my getting $1,000 on January 1st, 1924 — not a bad bargain with the money absolutely safe." It is doubtful that any other Hollywood star was ever quoted on peacetime Treasury bonds or was able to interest the public in them.

She influenced the public in other ways. Her agents claimed that she "ruined 50 men, made 150 families suffer." When she appeared in *The Clemenceau Case* the tabloids quickly reported that a defendant on trial for attempting to kill his wife blamed Theda's film for inspiring him to commit the deed. She even had, supposedly, a real vampire incident of her own, although she regularly denied any similarity to her characters. Apparently a young man committed suicide in her dressing room because she spurned his love. The Maharajah Gaekwar of Baroda, India, had been visiting in Paris and had been

Bara appears at a dedication ceremony during the war (courtesy of the Academy of Motion Picture Arts and Sciences).

drawn by the charms of the vampire actress. To show his appreciation he gave her a "wonderfully wrought" snake bracelet containing some Indian poison. When the actress showed the young suitor the secret spring which released the poison from the mouth of the hollow gold snake, he seized the bracelet, placed the snake on his lips, and died "at her feet." While this story in the *Peoria Journal* in 1915 was based on no facts, Archie Bell noted, "Theda, you're a wise little girl; when it comes to providing what newspapers and magazines know as 'copy,' you are in a class by yourself."

By 1918 Theda Bara was considered such an expert on vampires that she was subpoenaed to give "expert testimony on vampires and the psychology of vampiring" in a Los Angeles murder trial. One George Martinez was accused of throwing his wife out their apartment window to her death. His defense attorney tried to prove that the deceased was not Mrs. Martinez but rather Rosa Aguilar, the very beautiful "vampire of Sonora town ... who ruled imperiously at the social functions of the Plaza and parts of Chinatown." Rosa supposedly lost her heart to Martinez — a no-no for vampires — and threw herself out the window when spurned. Theda was to have been called on to "describe the mental tendency toward suicide of a thwarted vampire." Whether or not the trial occurred and, if it did, whether Theda appeared is unknown. However, what is certain is that the public actually took her for a vampire.

Some even took her vampire nature from her physiognomy. In 1916 a New York medical quack declared that he had "never gazed into a face betraying such wickedness and evil — that Miss Bara belongs to what we term the wide-faced, muscular type of people whose bones are slender and small, and who are governed by the same muscular system as the serpent. They have the feline temperament, deliberately taking pains to inflict suffering on others." Another medical quack tried to defend the vampire: "Theda Bara has a very wicked, cruel and evil face, but she is not wicked, cruel and evil. Unlike the gullible, who never scent evil, she has a sense of evil. This, evidently, is a gift which the motion picture producers failed to recognize."

Her most lasting cultural contribution, however, was not her depictions of evil but rather her influence on American sexual mores. It was she, for example, who helped to make the use of cosmetics socially acceptable. How do the social historians view her influence?

Kevin Starr declared that "Americans were in a transitional state regarding their willingness overtly to acknowledge sexuality as a primary force in human affairs ... [and] Theda Bara helped this point of view to articulate itself."

Frederick Lewis Allen, speaking of that "prelude [to the 1920s] time," May 1919, includes her among half-a-dozen movie stars that a typical middle-class American family would go to see. On the other hand Mark Sullivan's six-volume history with heavy emphasis on the entertainment field makes only a single mention of her.

Samuel Eliot Morison, one of the deans of American historiography, credits Theda Bara — along with increased knowledge of sexual hygiene, the mass production of the automobile, jazz dancing and a declining fear of the stern Old Testament God — with helping to crumble the Protestant ethic: "Moving pictures were becoming more attractive and lascivious; the sight of Theda Bara very lightly clad, in close and luscious embrace with a lover, could not help but be suggestive." In the same vein, Lloyd Morris' excellent book *Not So Long Ago* (quoted in Bodeen) describes the "baby vamp":

In millions of American homes the fumes of incense came to signify, not the presence of mosquitoes, but the anticipated arrival of a male caller. The undershot Bara-look was either an ominous hint of danger, or a half-explicit promise of pleasure, depending upon the degree of emancipation achieved by the female who practiced it.

For a while, feminine ambulation was slithery, and feminine posture languorous. An exotic pallor was cultivated by the most robust; necklines dropped alarmingly; and in a sudden wave of black that crossed the land, nubile girlhood appeared to be adopting universal mourning. Miss Bara made voluptuousness a common American commodity as accessible as chewing gum. And when this had been done, the old order was exposed to successful assault.

Not only the old order was assaulted, but the language was assaulted as well. With the success of the vampire movies Bara's name became a part of everyday language. A March 1920 article in the *New York Times* concerning London described the city as a "vampire city" which had taken a "Theda Bara role" draining Britain of its best youth. Two years earlier the *Cleveland Leader* described the complete assimilation of "Theda Bara" into the English language: "To be a vampire now is to be a Thedabara, and vice versa. You often hear your highbrow friends remark of an actress giving a 'bara-esque performance,' or having a 'bara role.' And in the poolroom... you'll hear some smart chappie characterizing his lady fair as a 'regular Theda.'"

There were the inevitable look-alike and letter-writing contests sponsored by Fox. In Cleveland a winner of a look-alike contest was offered a prize of five dollars. Another contest, in Louisville, offered two free tickets to *Carmen* for the best letter of a thousand words on the following topic: "Can a woman who faithfully presents the intricacies of this deep, dark character upon the stage, be, in real life, the innocent, charming and lovable creature which every man holds as an ideal wife?"

Three examples of entries into the Louisville contest show how well the Fox publicity had paid off. "Just think what she could make a husband suffer if he happened not to dance exactly correct when she pulled the string," wrote one entrant. Another echoed a similar sentiment: "You see, Miss Bara has a reputation to live up to. Each vampire picture must be more vampirish than the other, and that means that she's bound to acquire the 'vampire' habit. I

Two publicity images from the height of Bara's career (courtesy UCLA Arts Library, Special Collections).

want to see her as 'Carmen' because she's out to outvampire herself. But marry her? Never!" A third summed up prospective husbands' fears most succinctly: "I would not marry her because she knows and can carry out her vampirish instinct too easily."

The strangest bit of publicity was found in *Photoplay* in February 1916, in a recipe for a "Theda Bara Sandwich." The recipe included toast, minced ham, mayonnaise, pimiento and sweet pickles, suggesting "something spicy and peppery for the world-renowned vampire," a sandwich "that bites a little and says 'more.'"

As was typical of the early stars, Bara was demanding and very hard to work with. She wanted things done her way and rejected the very idea of direction. In those days many other Hollywood workers were annoyed by that attitude with the result that many a star lost his or her glory simply by not getting along with the crew.

Frenchman Ferri, who was an extra as a policeman in *The She-Devil*, recalled her as anything but dominant. He saw her as spoiled, self-centered and insecure: "Suddenly the star's forehead is creased with a frown, a darkening brow, a pointing finger, the finger of a badly raised child: 'Director! I don't want this girl near me!' orders Theda, out of her perpetual fear of seeing on the screen with her the face of someone younger and prettier. The director understands, and as the charming young lady leaves the scene, two impossibly ugly heads come in to frame the star as a double buffer. 'How charming it will be like that!' says the pacified star."

Others, including Al Selig, saw the soul of generosity, having "seen her write hundreds of checks for $10 or $25 in answer to a plea of some unknown fan," and the daughter of one of her maids recalled that Theda was "a very compassionate lady." In this same vein, in 1926 she caught a young female burglar in her home. Grabbing the thief by the arm in a darkened room, she made her drop the loot, consisting of furs, an evening dress and some fine lingerie. The *Los Angeles Times* quoted her as saying, "She was very young and little, and she promised to go straight," and apparently Theda believed her for there is no mention of calling the police.

Bara claimed that "Every mother and every minister owes me gratitude because every picture in which I appear has a clear moral. I am saving hundreds of girls from social degradation and wrongdoing." Well, perhaps.

NINE.
Vamped to Death

*T*heda Bara had skyrocketed to fame based on one movie and had put the Fox studio on a sound footing. Its 1914 income of $272,401 was microscopic compared to its 1915 take of $3,208,201, and the numbers just kept rising. In 1919, Bara's last big year, the studio made $9,380,883. Assuming that the public had an unquenchable thirst for Theda the vamp, Fox ground out movies monthly for three years and quickly wore the role to death.

Not only did the vamp formula suffer, but Theda's career suffered as well. Though she eventually did other dramatic roles besides the siren routine, it was too late. By the time *Kathleen Mavourneen* was released in 1919 it was impossible to accept Theda Bara as an innocent Irish peasant girl. Even the *New York Times*, in its February 1916 calculation of viewers, wondered if the public might not tire of her. But reviewers generally treated Theda kindly, crediting the actress with the ability to rise above the inferior material with which the Fox organization saddled her. For a while, Bara succeeded in spite of the garbage given her.

Overuse of the vamp formula was what killed the fad, but other factors were at work as well. The end of World War I brought change and unleashed a new generation of more sophisticated audiences on movie theaters. They regarded the Fox stars as out of date, out of touch. They demanded more subtle motives for the passions they saw on the screen. According to Alex Walker, "they were looking for ... neuroses as well as sex." Sex and sin were still hot topics, but they were no longer viewed as all bad.

The very role of the vamp, being evil incarnate, could not last because the younger audiences revolted against such a vicious concept. Moviegoers were seeing with different eyes, eyes that had seen many changes. During the war, great numbers of women left their homes to work. These women resented the vamp, a woman who lived well without any visible means of support and under no obligation to get a job.

A Fool There Was had set the vamp's character in film audiences' minds as the woman who is irresistible to men and revels in their destruction through her perverted "love." She lives a life of luxury and decadence, with liquor and wild parties her major pastimes, aside from the seduction of men. *Fool* acquainted audiences with Theda Bara and her special kind of vamping. Her dark, richly beautiful face and hair captured the imagination of her public and they readily equated her dark beauty with sin and destruction. She became famous for her eyes, which in intense moments of vamping would widen incredibly to a degree that appears comical to modern audiences. In 1915, however, her look was deadly to males, and women tried to imitate her. Thus was the first "star" created. The *Dramatic Mirror* reviewed her performance as that of "a neurotic woman gone mad. She has enough sex attraction to supply a town full of normally pleasing women, and she uses it with prodigal freedom." Others failed to see the vamp quite as seriously as that. Lew Sarett, in *Motion Picture* in 1918, parodied the Kipling poem that had inspired *Fool* in "The Ballade of a Rheumatic Vampire," and in an obviously Cajun dialect described her as a

> … Vampire-bug —*mon Dieu!* I nevaire seen-me-yet!
> Got beeg brown eye lak wan seeck calf, she's roll lak
>   bad coquet;
> Got figure lak wan circus hoss; she's walk lak snak'
>   what's grease';
> Her clothes dey was so t'in an' small dey fall off if
>   she sneeze'!

Another saw her not as a vamp but as a money-maker created by Fox and foisted on the public:

> A Fool There Was, and he paid his Coin,
> To a dark-eyed Dame, from the Ten-der-loin.
> He took her out to a West Coast Town,
> Dressed her up in a Form-fit Gown,
> Filled her Eyes with Bel-la-Don-na,
> And said, "Now Kid, forget your Hon-na,
> For, Hence-forth, you're a scar-let Scamp -
> She signed his Con-tract, for she was Meek,
> He made her Famous with-in a Week;
> And when I tell you his Pro-fits, you'll
> A-gree that, perhaps, he wasn't a Fool.

Fox was, of course, very much aware of the financial possibilities of his new actress, and he took advantage of the box office appeal created by her first role. Of her next 39 films for Fox, only six cast her in a non-vamp role.

It is often asserted that Fox used her up. It should be noted, however, that while she did make Fox a very wealthy man, her career was relatively short while others were still playing before the camera.

A two-photo publicity set with Theda in extravagant finery (courtesy UCLA Arts Library, Special Collections).

When the Bara-vamp role declined, so did the Fox Company's profits. William Fox got nervous. When Theda started in 1914 she was paid $75 a week. By 1919 she was making $4000 a week. When she demanded $5,000 a week, Fox balked. Her films were costing $60,000 each to produce, and box office receipts were declining. Having already milked the Bara image for all it was worth (even to the extent of editing and reissuing her early films in 1918), Fox let Theda Bara go when her contract expired. Fox already had another money-maker in his stable: cowboy Tom Mix (1880–1940), whose films were easier, quicker and cheaper to produce and brought in more and more dollars.

The circumstances of Theda's departure are not completely clear. Apparently she had a breakdown. To the press she stated that her health was bad and that she needed a rest. "Five practically uninterrupted years of vamping had drawn my nerves pretty taut. I seldom had longer than a week between pictures, and even that was not my own…" Hardly happy about Fox's treatment of her, Theda added, "I had been getting wretched stories and studio life was beginning to get on my nerves.... Mr. Fox seldom came to the studio—he was busy at the home office. I only saw him a few times a year."

Was Bara sexually exploited by William Fox? The road to screen success via the casting couch is an old cliché that probably has a strong factual basis, though we may never know how many of the old stars were sexually involved with a studio chief. At the time such things would have been covered up, yet hints of such early-day goings-on have surfaced. An old-time star, Fifi D'Orsay (1904–1983), told the owner of the Hollywood Poster Exchange that while she was under contract to Fox as a 24-year-old in 1929 she was very much involved with the Fox president, Winfield Sheehan (1883–1945). Known to the public for her French floozie roles and widely identified as the protégée of Will Rogers, D'Orsay was actually Mr. Sheehan's protégée.

She was certainly not the only one. In the industry's early decades it was perhaps even more common for women to be sexually exploited than in later days. Rare was the woman who was allowed to rise to the top because of talent alone. Bette Davis was one, but for many others there were other routes. Men did not have such a problem, generally getting their positions more through talent, yet the William Desmond Taylor murder case of 1922 proves that homosexual activity was not unknown in the film world. It took 70 years for all of the details of that crime to be revealed. A thick cloak of secretiveness protected Hollywood sexual reputations in Theda Bara's day.

After Fox let Theda go, she tried to go back to the stage. Broadway producer A. H. Woods (1870-1951) produced, albeit off-Broadway, *The Blue Flame*, the supernatural tale of an unemotional scientist (John Varnum, played by Alan Dinehart) whose fiancée (Ruth Gordon, played by Theda Bara) becomes the guinea pig for his newly invented life-restoring ray after she is killed by lightning.

Bereft of soul, the resurrected Ruth becomes a sultry, slinky succubus who lures innocent men to their doom. As theatrical historian Edwin Bronner describes it, "Before her exotic blandishments have run their course, the audience is treated to a comprehensive catalog of vice, 1920s style, including seduction, burglary, murder, blasphemy, the cocaine habit, infidelity and white slavery." To *New York Tribune* reviewer Percy Hammond, Theda as Ruth was "an actress who is so bad that she entertains rather than affronts. Some of her more heated passages are delivered with all the fervor of a lady demonstrating pancake flour in the food section of the department store.... The audience was something between reverent and amazed."

Though painfully bad, outside of New York the play was a smash hit, and Mark Sullivan recalled that "the curiosity to see it ... was so great that frequently riots were threatened." In Boston it was sold out for two weeks. To Theda it looked as if a new success had sprung forth. Interviewed by the *Boston Sunday Post*, she remarked, "During my career as a screen star I have felt the limitations of the camera, as all must have felt then who worked in the silent drama. It is, therefore, for the purpose of gratifying my own ambition to meet the public on a more personal basis that I accepted Mr. Woods' offer to present me in the spoken drama."

The contract Woods gave her would enrich her by $1500 plus half of the weekly net profit; for the Boston performance, for example, she received $10,700 — not an inconsiderable sum in those days. The press was friendly, the following report from one Boston paper being typical:

In costume for *The Blue Flame* (courtesy of the Academy of Motion Picture Arts and Sciences).

> One of the sights of [Boston] these days is the arrival and departure of Theda Bara from the Majestic. In the neighborhood of the stage door when she is due gather hundreds of the curious and it has been necessary to call out the police reserves on several occasions to take care of the crowd. If it were not for the weather conditions [at her latest performance] the crowd would probably have numbered thousands. Theda was originally booked to go to and from the theatre in a coach drawn by several pair of milk white horses. This idea was abandoned. The limousine she uses attracts enough attention....
>
> The debut of Miss Bara on the legitimate speaking stage in a dramatic play has proven a revelation to theatredom. While it is incomprehensible to show people why film fans who saw the famous screen vamp from 25¢ downward will pay $2 or more to see her in person in a speaking piece, that fact remains nevertheless. The strength of the Bara draw appears to be from among her picture admirers.

To keep her on the road Woods offered every concession, including a private railroad car sumptuously furnished, such as the great Bernhardt had enjoyed. Washington and Pittsburgh were triumphs after Boston. When asked to what he ascribed the phenomenal Bara box office pull, Martin Herman of the Woods office answered, "The most important fact is overlooked.

Two wartime photographs. *Top:* Shaking hands with two soldiers; *bottom:* visiting wounded soldiers (both photos courtesy of the Academy of Motion Picture Arts and Sciences).

William Fox spent $2 million to make Theda Bara the best known picture actress in the world. The result of that now is being reaped by Miss Bara."

But Bara wanted to conquer Broadway, to have "an opportunity to play the sort of part the public wants to see me play." On March 15, 1920, she opened at the Shubert Theatre. The critics engaged in a panning orgy. Josephine Victor, the wife of *Times* executive Frank Reid, was there in one of the best seats. Nearly 50 years later she recalled, "I was so unhappy for the star. We were in the first row but we could just about hear her. Perhaps it was stage fright, opening night and all that, poor dear, but she just had the tiniest voice."

Alexander Woolcott of the *New York Times* gave a variant view: "She is pretty bad, but not bad enough to be remembered always. Indeed, she has a very pleasant voice. She speaks her lines distinctly. And she displays a fine self-possession which enabled her to proceed last evening with unflinching gravity even when the audience lost control of itself and shook with laughter.... The play is a terrible thing.... If it were not for Miss Bara it would be easy to predict a phenomenally brief existence for [it]. It is the kind of play that, under normal circumstances, could not run a week in New York."

Bud Schulberg, whose father worked for Adolph Zukor, also experienced that opening night: "The first time she opened her mouth, they laughed. *This* was the irresistible vampire against whom the Church and an organized group of outraged housewives had fulminated as a threat to the established order? *This* was the Serpent Woman? Cleopatra and Salome incarnate? At the first sound of her childlike piping, cruel laughter ended her career."

Heywood Broun (1888-1939) of the *New York Tribune* added his opinion: "At the end of the third act Miss Bara said that God had been very kind to her. Probably she referred to the fact that at no time during the evening did the earth open and swallow up the authors, the star and all the company. However, it has often been remarked that the patience of Heaven is infinite. Still, as we remember it, Jonah was eaten by a whale for much less."

In the same paper another columnist, who regularly signed himself "FPA," punned, "Perhaps *The Blue Flame* is not a perfect title for Miss Bara's play. Why not: *Tenting on the Old Vamp Ground*?"

Theda herself recalled to Alan Brock, "We had every reason to expect a huge success in New York after the very responsive pre–Broadway tour, but — well — it was just not in the stars for us. Those critics ... those naughty critics — they completely tore the play apart. They could see only the wickedness and none of the good; they wrote our play was hackneyed — that I overacted hopelessly. So, of course, *The Blue Flame* was quickly extinguished." Brock recalled that there was "a trace of pain in her voice. It was obvious that her acceptance by the New York critics would have meant more to her than all the motion picture acclaim."

After 48 performances the play closed in New York.

After the failure of *The Blue Flame* Bara probably turned, for a while at least, to vaudeville, for a 1921 issue of *Theatre* contains her portrait with the caption, "Not so wicked after all, is she? Certainly not, judging from this picture which shows the Queen of the Vamps as she appears in vaudeville." Aside from this reference there is no other evidence that she attempted anything else at the time.

The end of the Fox-Bara relationship signaled a dying gasp for the vamp. The role was dying of ridicule, "Kiss me, my fool" having lost its solemnity and become a camp catchphrase for the romantic flippancy of the young. Others tried to fill Theda's shoes — Nita Naldi, Pola Negri, Dorothy Dalton (1894-1972), Barbara LaMarr (1896-1926) — to no avail. Fox himself tried to groom Betty Blythe (1893-1972), a protegée of J. Gordon Edwards, as a new vamp. He starred her in *Queen of Sheba* in 1921, but they had a falling out. She married, left Fox and went to Europe to make films, notably the 1925 English production of *She*. Ironically, Fox tried to squeeze some more mileage from the role and he remade *A Fool There Was* in 1922 with Estelle Taylor. It flopped.

In the 1920s came such stars as Alice Terry, Norma Talmadge (1893-1957), Norma Shearer (1900-1983), Florence Vidor (1895-1977) and the legendary Gloria Swanson (1897-1983). These were women of a more cynical and frivolous world than that mystically sinful and torrid one inhabited by the older star. The era also brought forth the flapper girls: Joan Crawford (1908-1977), Colleen Moore (1902-1988), Constance Bennett (1904-1965), Marion Davies (1897-1961), and Louise Brooks (1906-1985) with her quality of "unique fatality." With their bouncing insouciance they upstaged the exotic vamps.

In April 1916 Theda Bara had told the *Chicago Press* that she had "ambitions. This work is just my severe training school, a groundwork upon which I intend to build a structure that will be lasting.... I want to be a tragedienne on the speaking stage." Unfortunately, her contract with Fox ended about the same time that her popularity with the public began to wane. By the 1920s Theda Bara was no longer a mysterious, dangerous lady, but a caricature of a foil to prewar morality. The new morality scoffed at a vampire's threats to hearth and home, for the war had changed public attitudes toward marriage and family. The early films of DeMille, such as *Old Wives for New* (1918) and *For Better or Worse* (1919), with their emphasis on glamour and extra-marital bed-hopping, had begun to undermine Theda the vamp's hold on the public during the war years. So by 1920 Gloria Swanson reclining in DeMille's bathtub had replaced Theda Bara's exotica.

Both Bara and Swanson were unclothed; the difference was in where they were unclothed. Swanson was unclothed realistically in a bath whereas Bara had to journey to ancient Egypt. Audiences acutely tired of the war were interested in the present and had no use for the past — especially the distant past.

With the postwar prosperity in America the people wanted to be shown how to enjoy this new phenomenon, not how to escape to a distant past.

The vamps were no longer the central figures in films but sideline villainesses. Now, as villainesses, they found themselves punished at the end of the drama by the tender, generous (in short, sympathy-evoking) love heroine. Compared to the new woman of the world created by Cecil B. DeMille, the vamp seemed crude and old-fashioned. After all, as Alexander Walker reported, DeMille took the vamp's wardrobe and toilette, where her servants prepared her for sexual battle, and "domesticated it by making the bathroom, where sexual charms are displayed, and the bedroom, where desires are fulfilled, into the popular focus of his early films." Sex, as exotic and "not quite in," had become an Americanized frolic. What had been serious, heavy with consequences and potentially dangerous was now simply fun.

The vamp tradition was swallowed up in the ideal exemplified for American womanhood by Greta Garbo and Marlene Dietrich — the femme who is fatale, but chiefly to herself. This woman of the world, displaying her neuroses as well as her sexuality, was alluring and driven, to be sure, but she herself suffered while making others do their share of suffering.

In 1927 Clara Bow (1905-1965) starred in Clarence Badger's film of Elinor Glyn's *It* and established, as "The IT Girl," an aggressive new sexual symbol of the times. Unlike Theda Bara's world, sex on the screen (and off it, too), went with some kind of job, the kind that a store clerk or secretary could see herself in and so identify with the girl on the screen. When it ceased to be a full-time pursuit in itself, screen sex went from the portentous to the flirtatious, and, as Walker puts it, "the vamp who sucked men's blood gave way to the flapper girl whose only aim was to 'snap a trap on a sucker's bank roll.'"

The final blow to the vampire came from Mae West (1892-1984), whose *Sex* (1926) and *Diamond Lil* (1928) not only vulgarized the old boudoir-toilette-preparation scenes with her exchanges of sexy banter with her chuckling black maids, but led audiences to an open amusement over an honest, broad and humorous presentation of sex. The vamp simply could not compete with that.

TEN.

Wedding Bells and Career Death Knells

*T*heda Bara might have lost some of her power to attract at the box office, but some of the world still found her noteworthy. Early in 1920 newspapers reported rumors that she was, variously, in a sanitarium, manufacturing men's trousers, and engaged to an evangelist who would not permit her to act in vampire roles. In February and August 1920 the papers reported her marriage to Tom Bodkin, former manager of non-champion boxer Frank Moran and manager of a musical comedy, "The Sweetheart Shop." The marriage was supposed to have taken place in either Pittsburgh or Montreal; the reporters were never really sure, which was appropriate since the story was fiction. In mid–1921 Bara was reported to have written a book, *Vampire or Woman*. In late 1923 a rumor circulated that she was broke because she sold off some of her art collection. The sanitarium, clothier, evangelist and author stories were ignored, but she heatedly denied the rather odd Bodkin marriage story and her attorney took care of the tales that she was out of money.

In 1915 she had remarked to *San Francisco Chronicle* reporter Walter Doyle that she could never find happiness in marriage. "I would be ever afraid," she revealed, "that my husband would see in me the vampire of the screen, the siren who used her charms to impel men to their doom." In private life she was not the vampire, but rather a home-loving woman who lived quietly with her parents and siblings in an apartment at 500 West End, New York, until her grand move to Hollywood and an eventual happy marriage. She was fond of sausages, corned beef and cabbage. She never went to parties because, as she said, "I didn't have the time." For one who had any man at her beck and call on the screen, her private life was a model of discretion, unblemished by any public scandal or misbehavior.

In April 1921 the papers announced that she and recently divorced Fox director Charles Brabin were about to tie the knot. But another Bara illness intervened — she was reportedly on the verge of a nervous breakdown — and she soon left for Europe to visit her sister. Some of the press concluded that Theda's having "at last been vamped herself" were just rumors. While in Europe, she saw her sister married in London to Frank Getty, a New York newsman. When she returned to New York reporters saw Brabin kiss her when she disembarked. This resurrected the rumors, which Brabin characterized as "all tommy-rot." They were "not going to get married, and there's nothing to hide. [We're] just good friends" he asserted emphatically. Mildly he asked, "Can't a chap kiss a young lady when she returns from Europe [without being] married?" But on Saturday, July 2, 1921, just before Theda's thirty-sixth birthday, the couple drove up to Greenwich, Connecticut, and were secretly married before a justice of the peace. Theda later reminisced to historian Bodeen, "Neither of us had ever been on time in our lives. So I thought, 'I'll shampoo my hair.' I did. And then bless you if the man wasn't actually punctual. I had to stick up my wet hair under my picture hat, and sneezed throughout the ceremony."

As reporter Doyle then saw it, "This woman of the screen who a few years ago made these solemn statements has picked as her mate for life possibly the one man in all this world who has seen her more than anyone else in the roles in which she has shown.... [As her director in *Kathleen Mavourneen* and *La Belle Russe* he] has drilled her in her portraiture of the role of the vampire.... This man is not afraid of the tigress of the film.... Theda Bara feared the thoughts of the men who had seen her only on the screen.... Yet it was the man who knew her best, in the camera's eye and away from the studios, who led her to the altar." Doyle concluded, "Theda Bara, whose screen love was her business, found real love within the gates of the studio, where only mimicry is supposed to abide."

The couple honeymooned on the Bay of Fundy, then in the wilds of Nova Scotia. They bought a tract of land there for a summer home and returned to New York City. Soon after they moved to California, he to direct and she to become a housewife.

Brabin had been a movie pioneer. Born in Liverpool in 1883, he was well educated and had worked first as a hotel clerk and then as a traveling salesman before landing a role in George Ade's *The College Widow*. Other plays and stage management followed. In 1908 he played Abraham Lincoln, his first movie role, in an Edison film. The manager of Edison productions, a Mr. Plimpton, was impressed with Brabin's knowledge, taste and gentle, artistic nature. Plimpton put him in charge of props and sets. In 1910 he was given a chance to direct in Edison's *The Man Who Disappeared*. Direction became his life.

Brabin switched to Fox and became a master of serial direction, starring Pearl White (1889–1938) in ten serials in the three years she was with Fox. In those precolor days most of his films were distinguished by pictorial beauty.

Top: The Brabins on horseback; *bottom:* Theda and the less aquatically inclined Charles at the beach (both photos courtesy UCLA Arts Library, Special Collection).

After marrying Theda, the tall, hawk-nosed, virile Brabin moved from Fox to Universal to direct Universal's *Driven*, one of the best Southern mountaineer films, cited by the *New York Times* as "a throbbing narrative ... in which a mother betrays her husband and two sons to save her youngest boy." From there he went to Goldwyn to direct *Six Days*, starring Corinne Griffith.

Contented for two years, the former vampire took to marriage and made her husband the focus of her life until 1923 when they decided, while at their vacation home, to do a remake of Longfellow's "Evangeline" in its own locale.

In 1919 Miriam Cooper, the actress who had gone on record as despising Theda, had starred in Fox's successful film version of the poem. *Variety* concluded: "Theda is said to hold the impression she can show Miriam a few wrinkles about playing the Evangeline role, and incidentally prove to her former employer, Fox, there are some hefty kicks left in the Bara draw, even though indications are not lacking that her power at the box-office has waned." For some reason Brabin's *Evangeline* did not materialize. Theda got the chance to upstage Miriam Cooper, something which the latter would naturally have thought impossible on the face of it.

After her brief hiatus, it was reported in October 1923 that Theda was considering a return to the stage under Woods' direction, but this never came about and she actually went on to a few more years on the screen. Her Broadway fling with *The Blue Flame* and the personal appearances which had followed had never lived up to expectations. Was she stuck with failures?

During this time the press was reporting that Theda would make a 12-week cross-country tour touching nine cities, including Chicago, Detroit, Louisville, Cincinnati and Atlanta. She would be taking a single reel to Lee Ochs' "larger film houses" preparatory to making "a single production of a spectacular nature." The tour guaranteed her $3,500 to $4,000 weekly, but there were no celluloid results. As a way of keeping her finger on the public pulse, when she appeared in a new city she always asked her audiences how they would like to see her on the screen — as a vampire or a good girl. Everywhere she was greeted with shouts of "Vampire!" from large majorities, with only a few dissenters preferring the good girl role. While Theda was in St. Louis during a tour, one candid person suggested that she play "a regular human being." Theda laughed and enthusiastically replied that she had always wanted to, and would this time. Commenting on this, *San Francisco Chronicle* movie critic "Scoop" Conlon observed that "the candid one hit the nail on the head.... If Miss Bara takes the candid St. Louisian's advice there is no reason why she cannot come back to her enviable place in the sun."

In November 1922, after five months of contradictory newspaper reports,

Opposite: The Brabins (third and fourth from left) and friends at a waterfall (courtesy of the Academy of Motion Picture Arts and Sciences).

David Selznick (1902–1965) announced that Bara would star in a film adaptation of a Eugene Walters play, *The Easiest Way*. Selznick and playwright-actor-producer David Belasco (1853–1931) expressed enthusiasm and Theda herself was ecstatic, but no production ever came. Early in 1923 it was reported that Bara was returning to the screen in Fred Jackon's *Madame Satan* under the direction of Selznick's Herbert Blaché. The *Los Angeles Times* headline shouted,

"Girls, Watch Your Step!
Theda Bara's Back in Film Capital and Says She Is
Going to Enter Pictures Again."

Photoplay magazine gushed over the announcement:

> Theda Bara, welcome back! The flapper died with short skirts. You may return to the screen and be received with open arms. We've missed you! It seems only yesterday that we waved farewell to the little ladies with one hand and with the other beckoned the pert sub-debs. Now the debs are dead; and it is, again, the day of the vamp. Negri, Nita Naldi, Barbara LaMarr. And — The First Lady of the purplish photoplays, La Bara, now making a new picture at the Selznick studios. She was on the stage for many months; then she found a screen story which suited her, and you'll soon be seeing her again. This time she is a very modern enchantress; seductive, of course, but with a heart and a soul and even a sense of humor....

Blaché directed five films in 1923 and one in 1924. None bore the title *Madame Satan*. The movie was finally made by Cecil B. DeMille in 1930 for M-G-M. Kay Johnson (1904–1975) played the role of the bored wife that had been mentioned for Theda.

It is not known which of these projects failed because Bara turned them down. When someone became a star he or she did not want to go downhill into lesser films. Some were glad to have a chance in a low-budget B picture, but others refused to consider them. The B studios could not advertise very much, so to be able to put up the name of a star like Theda was worth money in the bank and thus there was always work for formerly big stars with the B studios. Consequently when a star of the era abruptly stopped working, it was usually that person's own choosing. The old stars usually refused B work at first. Many of them later would have been glad to take a lesser role, but for most it was too late. Snobbery or a refusal to be sold short prevented many a chance at continuing work or staging a comeback.

Five months after the announcement of *Madame Satan,* in June 1923, rumors circulated that Bara would join her husband at the Goldwyn studio, where he was working on Elinor Glyn's *Six Days*, to star in Glyn's forthcoming *Three Weeks*. The *New York Times* seemed to substantiate the rumor in October, but again, nothing developed. Aileen Pringle was chosen for the Alan Crossland-directed farce.

The problem undoubtedly centered on Bara's vamp role, which made her the leading star of *Los Angeles Times* critic Grace Kingsley's "Live It Down Club," the subject of a story of how stars lived down their handicaps: "You remember the joke about Miss Bara's getting 'barah and barah?' That matter of clothes now, curiously enough, while everybody will go see the undressed actress, such undressing really in the long run does her no good. The public would accept Miss Bara in no other sort of parts. She really had to leave pictures and go on the stage to, so to speak, get her clothes back on." But even Kingsley was convinced in July 1923 that Theda was on the eve of a huge comeback.

In 1924 Theda Bara Productions was incorporated in an effort to restore the queen to her cinematic throne, but it never made a picture. Then the break came.

Early in December 1924 the Chadwick studio announced to the press that Bara had been signed to work on its forthcoming *The Unchastened Woman*, a domestic comedy drama written by Louis Anspacher which had done well on the stage with Emily Stevens in the lead. The story was of a woman who finds out her husband is unfaithful just before the birth of their child. Going to Italy, she becomes "the talk of Europe" but returns to teach her husband a much-needed lesson, and all is happy. Theda was given the leading role as Carolyn Knollys, a wife who vamps to save her marriage. Her costars were George Walsh, Wyndham Standing, John Miljan (1892–1960) and Eileen Percy (1899–1973).

One newspaper trumpeted, "So there you are. Theda has come through. Here's luck to all concerned." Another announced that "Miss Bara, one of the most exotic and picturesque personalities of the screen, will be given a splendid director and a notable cast, and every effort will be made to surround the star with settings, costumes and players adequate to her high place in the film world." A third paper greeted the news cautiously: "The return of Theda Bara to the silver sheet has been announced so many times, only to fade out, that I am rather cagey about making any prophecies about the latest announcement. [And as for James Young] he hasn't directed a picture in some time, so the comeback of the screen siren will be doubly interesting." A fourth tersely announced that "Theda Bara returns to the screen after an absence of seven years at the old Miller Theatre Tuesday night [March 16, 1926], in an adaptation of Louis K. Anspacher's stage success 'The Unchastened Woman.' The Hollywood film colony will welcome her back to the screen and also celebrate the reopening of the Miller Theatre."

A seven-reeler, the film appeared unsuccessfully in 1926. It was intended to please female audiences but failed because the character became so inane that no one could find her intriguing. Title dialogues was cut and altered, and scenes were spliced in ways which totally altered Theda's original perception

A striking pose from the early 1920s, between *The Blue Flame* and *The Unchastened Woman* (courtesy of the Academy of Motion Picture Arts and Sciences).

of the film, creating what one reviewer saw as a new Theda Bara who was "neither as devastating as the noted vampire of five years ago nor as interesting and human as the woman ... Miss Bara had longed to portray." Walsh, Miljan and Percy all went on to make many films through the next decade and beyond.

In *The She-Devil* (1918), Theda had played the role of a comedienne. When Archie Bell asked if the world was ready to accept her as such, she replied, "The world must realize that I'm not a terrible creature stalking over the earth; I merely play the parts that will entertain." She further stated, without giving specifics, that she had played comic roles in Australia and that everyone there thought of her as a comedienne rather than as a vampire. Once, in February 1919, she actually made a direct appeal to an audience in Los Angeles, where she spoke with "telling simplicity, but breadth of understanding, and warmth of human sympathy concerning her work," in the words of the *Examiner's* reporter. "Whenever I try to be a nice, good little thing, you all stay away from my pictures," she chided the crowd, further explaining that in real life she was "timid and reticent" rather than the screen vamp. Her audience, however, could not be persuaded and her non-vamp films failed to cause the sensation her vamp ones did.

Hal Roach (1892–1992) was attempting to make short-comedy stars of stage and screen performers whose luck had temporarily run out — Priscilla Dean and Lionel Barrymore (1878–1954), for example, as well as Theda, who was a good friend of Roach's wife Virginia. So on November 10, 1925, Roach persuaded Theda to make a comedy poking fun "at the now out-of-date intense adventuress role." Thus was born *Madame Mystery*, a farce comedy directed by Stan Laurel (1890–1965) and starring Theda Bara, Oliver Hardy (1892–1957) and James Finlayson (1887–1953). It came just before the first Laurel and Hardy movie, *45 Minutes from Hollywood*, was released at Christmas 1926. Bara approached the film with genuine delight, saying, "Vamping requires no artistry whatever. Comedy requires a real test of skill. There are such delicate nuances — such opportunities for subtlety. For me, henceforth, high comedy!" Released in 1926, this two-reeler turned out to be only hysterical slapstick.

Roach, for his part, had little luck with trying to remake performers; they had never been clowns and no longer had sufficient youth or doggedness to set about learning how to be. But for Hardy it was a godsend. He was playing a plug-ugly in support of Theda when the horse he was riding buckled under his weight on a sand dune. The incident struck the assembled crew as so funny that Hardy was permitted to revert to outright comedy, mainly in support of such Roach regulars as Charlie Chase (1893–1940) and the ailing Mabel Normand (1898–1930). Though he was still no more than a backup man, he was at least on the lot being directed by Laurel — who was sufficiently impressed, as it turned out, to team up with him.

For Theda Bara, it was the end of her film career. If her strategy had been to wait for a major film and to scorn lesser ones, it backfired and she had to live with the results. While her career was dying on the vine, her husband was growing even more successful. A master of camera technique, he often boasted that he had directed Pola Negri and had filmed her through a gauze placed on the camera, thus making her look absolutely gorgeous in a mysterious way. "I was never really enthused about her," he later reminisced to his dentist, "but I made her seem beautiful to the camera's eye."

After *Driven* and *Six Days,* Brabin began making *Ben-Hur* for Sam Goldwyn, a massive stage money-maker which Goldwyn had financed by mortgaging an unprecedented 50 percent of the film's future earnings. In January 1924 Brabin led his company to Rome and constructed enormous sets. The cameras rolled spasmodically and sluggishly for three months and then Goldwyn became part of the newly formed M-G-M. The first rushes to come back after the first half was filmed were disappointing. The next problem to disquiet the bosses was the incredible expense of the outsized sets, and other snags followed. Marcus Lowe, the new firm's president, was so upset by this profitless situation that he personally sailed to Italy with replacements including a new director, Fred Niblo (1874–1948). The new group soon had as much trouble as the old, so early in 1925 they were ordered back to California where the company could keep an eye on them. On a patch of empty land on La Cienega Boulevard in Los Angeles (at the present location of Fedco) they rebuilt the Colosseum set and reshot the picture. It was a serious blow to Brabin's career.

Brabin next went to First National in 1925 for *So Big,* with Colleen Moore; then back to Universal in 1926 for *Stella Maris* with Mary Philbin (1903–1993), who had just finished starring in *The Phantom of the Opera* with Lon Chaney, and then to M-G-M where he remained until his retirement in 1938.

In 1926 John Grierson, writing in *Motion Picture News,* called Brabin one of five "directors in Hollywood [who] have a consistent visual sense and a feeling for composition…. Their pictures are beautiful but soft." However, Grierson went on, "they indicate no great capacity to vary their sense of visuals from soft to hard, from gentle to brutal."

Between 1929 and 1934 Brabin continued directing several films a year. His output included *Bridge of San Luis Rey*, with Cisco Kid Duncan Renaldo (1904–1980), featuring a few minutes of talk; *The Ship from Shanghai*, reviewed as "no pleasure cruiser"; *Call of the Flesh*, with tango dancers Ramon Novarro (1899–1968) and Renée Adorée (1898–1935); *The Great Meadow*, which "awed small audiences"; *The Singer from Seville*; *Green Meadow*; *City Sentinel*; and *Sporting Blood*, a winner with a rousing Kentucky Derby climax, which gave Clark Gable (1901–1960) his first top star billing.

Actually, Gable had gotten one of his first screen tests through Brabin's sister-in-law, Lori. Years later, she told a nurse at the convalescent home where she retired that Gable never acknowledged that boost. As a result she always resented him, and for various other reasons she never really cared for her director brother-in-law.

Brabin's 1932 film *The Beast of the City*, with Jean Harlow (1911–1937), began with a foreword by President Herbert Hoover and ended with a vice gang being mowed down by police. Harlow's biographer Curtis Brown quotes the *New York Times* reviewer: "She was a distinct asset to the racketeering melodrama that director Brabin endowed with vitality and realism."

Then there was *Washington Masquerade*, a failure with Lionel Barrymore, and then another failure with Lionel's sister Ethel (1879–1959). In 1932 Brabin was chosen as the director for *Rasputin and the Empress*, and the grandiose Ethel was chosen for the role of the Czarina Alexandra. This was the only time all three Barrymores appeared in the same film. On her first day Ethel told Brabin how happy she was to be working with him, but the sentiment was short-lived. Exasperated by what she considered Brabin's excessively slow pace, disgusted as usual at being directed at all and eager to get back to New York, she went to a studio telephone on a wall near the set and told Louis Mayer in tones which the entire company could hear, "See here, Mayer, let's get rid of this Brahbin or Braybin or what's his name." According to Barrymore biographer John Kobler, "Brabin immediately left the set and, at Ethel's suggestion, was replaced by Richard Boleslavsky, a Polish author reputedly knowledgeable about Russian royalty." Apparently Brabin never really recovered from the embarrassment of being pulled from that film. He may have had the last laugh, though for M-G-M took a loss thanks to high reshoot costs, and that was not warmly regarded by the company comptrollers, especially during the Depression.

After that failure Brabin's pride reportedly asserted itself and kept Theda from going back to the movies; in fact he nearly blackballed her, according to one of her acquaintances who related the story to Bob Coleman, owner of the Hollywood Poster Exchange. Whether this was true is open to speculation. In any case, however, M-G-M lost more stars than any other studio after the advent of the talkies. Having signed many foreign performers during the silent days, including, for example, Ramon Novarro and Greta Garbo (1905-1990), they found that these actors did not do well with sound. Some of the Americans they had hired, such as John Gilbert (1895–1936), were excellent melodramatic actors but did not have good voices. Warners, on the other hand, had more success, getting James Cagney (1899–1986), Edward G. Robinson (1893–1973), Joan Blondell (1909–1979) and Bette Davis (1908–1989) from New York. Not very attractive physically in some cases, they nevertheless were trained Broadway actors and actresses and did very well in Hollywood.

More successful for Brabin than *Rasputin and the Empress* was *The Mask of Fu Manchu*, a "lavish hokum" with Boris Karloff (1887–1969) and Myrna Loy (1905–). This 1932 film, which also starred Lewis Stone (1879–1953) and Karen Morley, was based on novelist Sax Rohmer's sinister and inscrutable Oriental villain, Dr. Fu Manchu, and combined a number of incidents from Rohmer's exotic thrillers. Karloff biographer Peter Underwood asked Rohmer for his opinion of the film and Karloff's characterization. "He told me that unfortunately he was in Egypt when the film was exhibited and he never saw it but he added: 'Boris Karloff would be an ideal choice for Fu Manchu.'"

Brabin's last films were *New Morals for Old*, a moderate success about youth versus age; *Day of Reckoning* and *Stage Mother*, two B pictures; *The Secret of Madame Blanche*, another "dip into the Madame X corn-bag" with Irene Dunn (1898–1990) playing a mother who takes the blame for a murder her unknown son has committed, mother and son discovering each other thereafter; and *A Wicked Woman*, the teary story of a mother who kills her sadistic husband to protect her children, keeping it a secret for ten years.

ELEVEN.

Bara, Brabin
and Beverly Hills

*T*he vamp took to domesticity as a vampire to blood. As attempted comebacks failed she became a Beverly Hills housewife and hostess. Throwing herself into the marriage as she had into her movies, she determined to learn (as when she researched Cleopatra's perfume) all there was to know about what was then called domestic science. In 1929 the *Los Angeles Times* happily reported on the success of her new research: "She has tastefully furnished and decorated a gem of architecture built at [632 North] Alpine Drive in Beverly Hills and has become an ardent devotee of literature. She is particularly interested in astrology and speaks with knowledge of literary classics and authors."

The house, built in the English cottage style, is much more spacious than is apparent from the street, with lots of light to balance the dark wood paneling. High vaulted ceilings boast chandeliers. Ornate scrollwork and medallions line the walls. Stained glass windows enhance a study. Three fireplaces, a bar in the style of an English pub, a small kitchen, a formal dining room, and an elevated stage or sitting area enclosed in glass and benefiting from the morning sun mark the rest of the interior. Surrounding all of this is a lovely yard. Her dentist, Dr. Edward Furstman, recalled that she had beautiful crystal, silver and china.

Her hobbies included collecting rare books and tramping through the wooded canyons that once were Beverly Hills. Over 20 years later Adela Rogers St. Johns, the Hearst Hollywood columnist, mentioned these same activities in a piece in *American Weekly*.

The Brabins' love deepened. Bodeen reported seeing birthday cards on which Theda had written such things as "To My Darling Mouchey-Mou — from Your Wiffle Tree." Charles returned the ardor. In May 1923, preparing to direct *Six Days*, he complained "I've been very lonesome without my wife." Ten years later Theda personally responded to a newspaper reader's inquiry about her whereabouts to the effect that "the wages of screen wickedness is domestic bliss." And St. Johns confirmed this by observing in 1950 that "they are still happily married."

Furstman recalled that they were "a very likable couple, an unusual combination." He described Theda as

> a very private person, dignified, every bit a lady. Every time I'd see her I had to tell her a bawdy story because she had a great sense of humor, but she was more or less withdrawn, I thought. While Charles, well, he was a gung-ho guy living life up to the utmost of his capacity. She was the practical one in the family because he was a pixie. I remember her getting a call at my office and it was from a hardware store in Beverly Hills. She came back and sort of sighed and sat in the chair and said, "Charles is up to it again." I said, "What do you mean, Mrs. Brabin?" (I never called her by her first name.) She said, "Well, he just ordered a lawn mower." "To cut the grass?" I asked. "Of course not," she said, "It's one he can sit on and ride around the yard. So I had to tell them to say 'Fine, Mr. Brabin, we'll have it up to the house' and then I canceled the order. We have no use for something like that."

She told her dentist many such stories. Apparently Charles would frequently buy things on their charge accounts, the stores would call her and she would cancel the order. "It wasn't senility or anything like that," recalled Furstman, "he just had champagne tastes when they had a beer pocketbook."

It wasn't just a bawdy story that Theda liked now and then. Ormsby Gumfudgin of La Crescenta reported that in 1946 he was persuaded by a photographer to pose nude for a set of pictures for Theda's boudoir. "I remember oiling my body for effect. I wasn't one of those muscular beach boys but maybe my youth was more important," he said.

As poor a track record as Hollywood has posted with regard to happy marriages, Mary Pickford and Leo Rosten may have been thinking of the Brabins (without naming them) when they penned the following impressions. From Pickford, married three times:

> I have always thought it amazing that, under the trying circumstances of the industry, so many marriages do survive. I wonder what would happen to doctors, dentists, factory workers and bankers if they found themselves exposed to the romantic conditions and temptations of the people of the screen and stage? To the actress the director shouts, "When you kiss him, mean it!" To the actor: "Put your arms around her and hold her close, as if you really loved her." Sometimes these sequences are repeated many times. Often they are between extremely vital and good-looking people, only rarely married to one another. The marvel is that happy and lasting marriages do exist among them. And there are a great many in Hollywood who go regularly and quietly to their own church or synagogue, who cherish a home and wife and children, who prefer their private lives to be kept out of the news.

And Rosten:

Theda in her Beverly Hills house, in front of her little stage with the patio just outside the window (courtesy of the Academy of Motion Picture Arts and Sciences).

Happy marriages and normal lives, in Hollywood as in Sheboygan, do not get publicity. And a good deal of Hollywood's amorous acrobatics is deliberately engineered by publicity officers and press agents. Romantic hoopla is unequaled as a method of "building up" personalities quickly; and the infatuations of fledgling actors and actresses are often plotted with as much care as their personal appearance tours.

At the beginning, however, gossipmongers gravely hinted that all might not be well: in December 1923 the *New York Morning Telegraph* speculated that the couple had "disagreed." This rumor was based on the omission of Theda's name on a telegram from director Brabin prior to his return from Italy. However, a few days later the same paper squelched the rumor by reminding readers of the photographs taken at the time of his departure showing "them in a fade-out that would do credit to the most ardent love story ever filmed. If the trouble has come," it concluded sagely, "it has come by radio or long distance." They were childless, as her goddaughter later observed, which was a good thing since Theda probably would have misplaced a child, so absent-minded was she.

The Brabins' lives blossomed with countless admiring friends. Theda was a well-known society matron, entertaining often at her Beverly Hills home, accompanying her husband to Europe, gadding about with her sister and doing charity work. After Mary Pickford, with whom Theda got along very well, gave up the leadership of the Beverly Hills social circle, the Brabins ascended the vacant throne. Theda's reputation was of a gracious, cultivated and witty hostess, famous for collecting antiques and interesting friends and for serving gourmet meals. Once when a star in a play, probably George Kelly's *Reflected Glory* starring Tallulah Bankhead, was ordering a dinner that made the audience salivate, George Cukor is reported to have whispered to his theater companion, Ethel Barrymore (probably without knowing of the cool relations between Ethel Barrymore and Charles); "Ah, pot luck at Theda Bara's!" This is not to say that Theda was the cook; her goddaughter recalls that though Theda's "parties were elegant, filled with fun and fine foods, she would rather die of starvation than cook." A man who was a guest at her parties concurred about the elegance: "They were the epitome of refinement, with champagne rather than hard liquor, and a general mix of 50 to 60 people from the film industry, local society and the upper strata." With other celebrities — Marion Davies, William Randolph Hearst, Thomas Ince (1880–1924), Wallace Reid (1891–1923), Rudolph Valentino (1895–1926) and Louise Brooks among others — the Brabins partied at the homes of such hosts as Max Linder (1883–1925) and Grace Darmand.

By the late 1940s the Brabins were giving only one party per year. No special occasion prompted it; it was merely an effort to repay all the people who had invited them to parties throughout the year. They had reached a position of being able to host only an annual event and their friends understood that. Theda always insisted that she did not want to give a party that was less than "top drawer," and the one a year that they could afford was the one they gave. Like the earlier parties, these continued the Brabin tradition of elegance.

It had not always been so. Around the time Theda's movie career ended she sold her home on West Adams Boulevard where she had never been too welcome, for movie stars were not considered worthy of admission into high

A pose in the garden of the West Adams home, autographed in 1920 (courtesy of the Academy of Motion Picture Arts and Sciences).

society or its neighborhoods. At the time West Adams between South Figueroa
and Western was Los Angeles' most elegant two-mile stretch; in fact Union
Oil founder Edward Doheny lived around the corner from Theda on Chester
Place. Her society neighbors were stricken in contemplating that, of all the
movie stars, *she* had dared to descend in their palatial midst. But when she
moved out to North Alpine her old neighbors would suffer a greater jolt: bois-
terous, hard-drinking Fatty Arbuckle (1887–1933), the Keystone Kops come-
dian, moved in wanting Theda's bedroom left "just as it is."

The attitude of her old Los Angeles neighbors was not atypical. Actors
and actresses for centuries were considered of low status, though in the late
nineteenth century the middle class seemed to treat them with respect. Her
neighborhood, however, was hardly middle class, and the old prejudices per-
sisted. Meanwhile, Beverly Hills which had been founded in 1906 and had
begun becoming a secluded resort after the Beverly Hills Hotel was opened in
1912, became the accepted location for film stars' mansions as the motion
picture industry grew. Even there some old prejudices prevailed. The *1935
Southwest Blue Book* was a case in point. As in Washington, New York or San
Francisco, Los Angeles' *Blue Book* was the final arbiter of who was who in society. Ramon Novarro had gotten in as a member of the Samaniegos family, but
when they were dropped, so was he; Antonio Moreno (1889–1967) got in
because of his wife, Daisy Canfield, but when she died he was out; Charlie
Chaplin, Douglas Fairbanks and Mary Pickford didn't make it; Mrs. Elizabeth
Fraser Lloyd was in but her son Harold was barred; Will Rogers, the Barrymores, Leo Carrillo (of an old Californio family), Norma Shearer and Marion
Davies (though her sister, Reine, and her father, Judge Bernard Douras were
listed) were among the outs. Anti-Semitism does not seem to have been a factor:
while Mr. and Mrs. Samuel Goldwyn (né Goldfish) were out, her equally Jewish
sister, Mrs. Constance Howard, was in. But Mrs. Charles Brabin was listed.

When Alma Whitaker of the *Los Angeles Times* asked Theda how she had
cracked the social walls, Theda laughed, "Perhaps I'm in for contrast. And
then, of course, I sinned only on the screen." Whitaker was not satisfied with
this non-explanation and asked the publisher of the book, Leonora King Berry,
about the apparent discrimination. Mrs. Berry replied, "Oh, I admire the picture people most sincerely, but for 36 years the *Southwest Blue Book* has had a
definite character — strictly society. So few of the screen people are society in
that sense. If I included them it would just be a different book altogether."
Upper crust Los Angeles society might have looked askance at the film colony,
but it got a well-deserved comeuppance from some other upper crusts. When
the Duke and Duchess of Alba visited California, their first request was to
visit Pickfair, and when Lord and Lady Mountbatten arrived on their 1922 hon-
eymoon, they refused invitations from the local society leaders and gave their
full time to the stars instead.

Two views of the Brabins' front porch: Theda in a thoughtful pose (*left*) and relaxing with Charles (both photos courtesy UCLA Arts Library, Special Collections).

At their New York address, 14 East 60th Street, the social whirl continued, though Charles suffered from head colds in the Eastern climate. The press was generally friendly, and Hearst's *New York Mirror and Journal* and Scripps-Howard's *New York World-Telegram* both gushed over her guest lists. The former, in February 1939, presented her now-forgotten guests: "the John Amens — she was Marion Cleveland, a daughter of President Cleveland; Mrs. J. Francis Clarke, one of Newport's most conservative matrons; Mr. and Mrs. James Blaine, another famous political name, and the Dick Knights — she the lady whose hair-do is as astonishing as Carrie Munn's hats," and so forth.

Theda's snaky gowns were replaced by the conservative look as she became a leading society figure, according to the *New York Post* in 1932. Her leadership status is oddly denied today by a spokesperson of the exclusive Beverly Hills Women's Club, yet Theda frequently spoke of this strictly exclusive club, where she seems to have confined her social life. She is not listed as a member of other high-toned Los Angeles, Beverly Hills or Hollywood organizations.

She did not belong to any church or synagogue, for both she and her husband were "irreligious as hell" according to one old friend. That is not to say, however, that she was completely devoid of a spiritual nature. The daughter of a maid recalls that if Theda lost anything "she would kneel in a corner of the room and pray to St. Theresa."

She was not listed by the *Times* as attending such social blowouts as the Olympiad Parties or the Los Angeles 151st anniversary party, both in 1932, but she liked to have fun. Her goddaughter, June Stanley (1922–1992) was the daughter of Henry Millarde, a Fox director, and June Caprice, a Fox star analogous to Mary Pickford. She recalled that her mother June and Theda, both of whom "would drink anything," would sometimes go to Tijuana in those Prohibition days, "get zonked" and drive back to Beverly Hills "laughing all the way." Theda was, according to Stanley, "very funny ... not for her jokes, just funny" and that on special days they'd "tootle around." Her dentist Edward Furstman remembered her as having "a fantastic sense of humor. She was sharp, she was quick, she was witty, she liked a good raunchy joke — nothing obscene, just bawdy–and this was in the very latter part of her life."

With two screen rivals she got along very well. Clara Bow and Mary Pickford followed her recommendation of a sales clerk at the I. Magnin's on Ivar and Hollywood in the late 1920s. Mrs. Castella Hicks had so pleased the ex-vamp that Theda always requested Mrs. Hicks as the saleslady to wait on her — as did subsequently the other two actresses, thus making Hicks the top salesperson in the store.

Bara got along very well with Charlie Chaplin but never cared for her mocker, W. C. Fields. Among those of the next generation, her goddaughter recalled that she thought Clark Gable and Cary Grant were "hunks" and utterly despised Joan Crawford. Apparently Theda regarded Crawford as a parvenue and knew that the publicly sweet relationship between Crawford and her adopted children was artificial.

She knew how to have a good time and was not afraid of being seen in public. She never "cried poor," even when they had lost their earlier wealth, according to one old friend. Mervyn LeRoy (1900–1987), the producer of *The Wizard of Oz* and other films, recalled that in the late twenties and early thirties "at the Coconut Grove, where the Hollywood crowds regularly gathered on Tuesday nights, we'd all have the same table, week after week. We went to see and be seen. You could look around and find the same faces in the same places — people like Wally Reid, Theda Bara, Ben Lyon, Nita Naldi, Barbara LaMarr, Mary Pickford, Charlie Chaplin, Douglas Fairbanks, all of them. Gus Arnheim's orchestra played for dancing, and there was a group of singers called 'The Rhythm Boys,' which included Bing Crosby, who supplied the vocals. There was no show — the audience was all the show we needed."

The future second wife of actor John Gilbert must have thought her loads of fun, for the young Leatrice Joy (1896–1985) once had a problem she took to Theda for solution. She was to have a date with Jack that night and wanted to be a knockout, but just didn't know what to do with her face.

"Theda Bara was delighted to help," recounted Leatrice to John Maxim. "I followed through the sitting room, stepping over velvet ottomans and fur rugs, through a beaded curtain into her boudoir. The walls were hung with cretonne prints and the air reeked of heavy musk. There was a caged snake on a shelf, which Theda would stroke in the presence of the press but which slept and ate bugs at all other times. Theda lived that way because she was expected to, but now she was just plain Theo Goodman enjoying a school-girl conspiracy. She seated me on a carved teakwood stool and went to work. When she was finished, I was something more than a knockout. I had rings of kohl darkening my eyes and a dusting of indigo. My mouth was arched in a deep-red cupid's bow and white powder accentuated my already pallid skin. As a final touch, Miss Bara took a rabbit's foot dipped in rouge and applied it to my earlobes.

"'What's that for?' Leatrice asked.

"The arch-vamp slid laughingly into a parody of herself. 'Zis is for earlobes pulsing vit ze blood of love. Zis means passion. Seething passion.'

"I wasn't entirely sure that seething passion was what I had in mind, but who'd know better than Theda Bara? I thanked her and went home to wait for Jack.

"My mother, Mary Zeilder, took one look at me and gasped. 'You're an actress, not a fancy woman. Go wash your face this instant.' Well, I had a doubt or two of my own, so I obeyed. All of Theda Bara's artistry was scrubbed away, but Mother and I both overlooked the pink ears.

"Jack arrived on time, and as far as he was concerned my well-scrubbed face was perfect.... [We went on our date but] at one point, I looked up and saw concern on Jack's face.

"'What's wrong?' I asked.

"'I think one of your earrings might be on too tight. You look as if you're getting an infection.'

"'My earring? I don't think so.'

"'Well, your earlobe has gone awfully red.'

"I suddenly remembered and burst into giggles. 'That's my seething pas-sion,' I told the blank-faced Jack. 'Couldn't you tell?' After I explained, describing my visit to Theda Bara's seraglio bedroom and Mother's reaction, we both laughed so hard we had to leave the dance floor.

"'Oh, Miss Joy,' he said, wiping away tears, 'you're a rare bird in this cock-eyed aviary. I hope you never leave it again.'"

Since they were later married — if only for two years (1923–1924) — it appar-ently had a good effect.

TWELVE.
Other Starts,
No Finishes

Theda tried her talents in fields outside of acting, one of which was writing. On November 17, 1925, the *Los Angeles Times* and the *San Francisco Examiner* both reported that she had written a book, *What Women Never Tell*, of which she said, "While it's partly autobiographical, thank goodness it doesn't depict me at the age of 7 speaking a piece before the Sunday school class. It's not a full confessional — only a part of what women never tell. One of the chapter heads is 'Men, Animal, Vegetable and Mineral,' and another is 'Let Her Who Is Without Sex Cast the First Stone.'" She was reported to be contacting publishers, but apparently none took the manuscript. A check of the *United States Catalogue* (July 1925-December 1927) and *Cumulative Book Index* (January 1928) turns up no mention of it.

Although she was finished as a screen actress Theda tried other ventures. She tried a few stage comebacks — sometimes writing her own plays, such as *The Red Devil* — and continually talked of a movie revival. It was not at the time a question of money or security; she had not been profligate with the sums she had made, and she had invested wisely. When the 1929 stock market crash occurred the Brabins were nearly wiped out but retained an annuity which paid them $3,000 a month — a very princely sum in those days, requiring an enormous principal. She also had a very loving, reliable husband, but she was impelled by some inner drive to return to acting.

On June 7, 1931, she made her stage re-debut at the Fulton Theatre in Oakland, playing the lead in Ernest Vajda's *Fata Morgana*. The author's theme was "that physical attraction may be something ephemeral." The story is of a mouse-like lad of 18 seduced by a jaded Budapest matron in a Hungarian farmhouse. It was written about half a dozen years earlier as a serious piece but was revised as a silly comedy, which the *Oakland Tribune*'s reviewer, Wood Soanes, described as "a bucolic burlesque with a European tang." He wrote that Theda "played her part hesitantly and more in the old cinema manner than

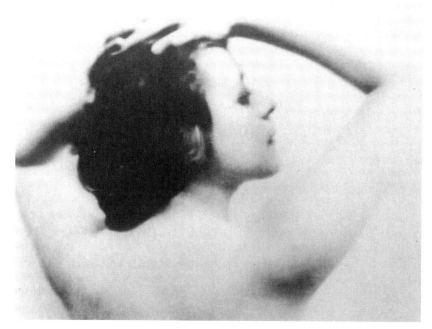

the newer school of naturalism" her scenes with the boy "were rarely effective and often unintentionally amusing." As to the overall effect of the play, he wrote that "Vajda [might] tear his hair in anguish ... but last night's performance did pass the evening pleasantly, and the first nighters found much to chuckle at."

Three years later, in May 1934, Bara took the stage again, this time in James Fagan's adaptation of Robert Hichens's *Bella Donna* at the Little Theatre of Beverly Hills for Professionals. The story is set on the Nile where an English courtesan fearing middle age falls under the spell of a local potentate whom she later tries unsuccessfully to poison, but is thwarted by his loyal physician. The *Los Angeles Times* reviewer, Katherine T. Van Blom, apparently enjoyed Theda's performance as the infamous Bella Donna, writing that she "was alluring throughout ... [but] at times her performance was marred slightly by lack of suavity, doubtless induced by first night nervousness, and there was a slight inclination toward older stage technics [*sic*], but her voice was throatily pleasing."

Her husband, to shelter her, and perhaps because he took note of things with a director's eye, often asked reviewers to "be kind." But reviews such as that for *Bella Donna* obviously encouraged her desire to return to the screen. Many times she was reported to be coming back: "It is very likely that before long she will begin production of a talking picture" (*Los Angeles Times*, January 1929); "Theda ... now is making voice tests" (*Photoplay*, August 1929); "Theda Bara is now content to be Mrs. Charles Brabin ... but you'll hear rumors of her screen return" (*Photoplay*, March 1932); and "A try at the talkies is possible. I still get fan mail" (United Press, April 1934). In June 1936 she gave a two-minute, obviously prepared interview to Woody Van Dyke of the Lux Radio Theatre in which this exchange took place:

VAN DYKE: I understand, Miss Bara, that you're going to make some radio appearances.
BARA: Yes, I am. And I'm also going to do some motion picture work.
VAN DYKE: Well, that's good news.
BARA: I'm considering an offer now, running through scripts and ideas. Oh, I just hope everyone will be as happy about another Theda Bara picture as I am. The public has been very good to me in the past.

Unfortunately, another movie was never to materialize.

Lori Bara, Theda's sister, after divorcing her first husband, married Ward Wing, a scenarist, in November 1927. She later divorced him after he deserted her during pregnancy; their daughter died soon after birth. All the while she

Opposite: Two views of a barer Bara in 1929, still beautiful at 44 (both photos courtesy of the Academy of Motion Picture Arts and Sciences).

made a living writing jungle thrillers for M-G-M, stories such as *Jungle Love* and *Tiger! Tiger!* She even joined her husband in Malaya in 1933 to produce her movie *Samarang*. Lori enjoyed the jungle, according to an interview she gave to the *New York World-Telegram*, seeing strange tribes of cannibals-turned-rat-eaters and fighting pythons but missing fresh milk. She never tried to use Theda's name to get ahead, always selling herself as an individual talent and never wanting to be connected to the Vamp.

Lori resented Charles Brabin, whom she blamed for her sister's retirement: "He's English, you see. You know how Englishmen are." Apparently the feeling was mutual, for goddaughter June Stanley recalled, "Uncle Charlie didn't like [Lori and] ugh! neither did I!"

Theda herself knew what Englishmen were like. In a letter to Hedda Hopper in June 1948 she referred to some young Englishman's indiscretion: "Recently in that sad tragedy you did not let the talented young man shed his responsibility in the so English male attitude of — le droit de seigneur…. You know, the Lord created the world in six days & on the seventh he rested!— and while He rested the English decided it was their natural heritage to take over! Don't mistake me, I have many English friends whom I love dearly — & I have a fatuous adoration of Churchill — but the English male attitude toward women was succinctly summed up in Lady Asquith's 'My education cost about the price of my father's oysters!'"

In her last two decades Theda still hoped for a movie revival, continuing to list herself as "at liberty" in the casting directories, traveling, going to an occasional Hollywood party, enjoying a happy marriage and granting an occasional interview. She never forgot the fans who made her a star. In August 1929 *Photoplay* printed her home address with an invitation to fans to write her there. This gesture was almost unheard of.

This symbiotic loyalty was not limited to her fans. Bara revealed her respect for her friends in a 1954 interview with impresario Alan Brock:

> I tactfully brought up the name of Mrs. Patrick Campbell, Miss Bara was ecstatic in praising the legendary actress. It was seldom that I had the chance to hear such praise from one female star about another. To Miss Bara, her friend was incapable of doing wrong. Her unfailing courage, effervescent wit, her artistry, redeemed her every sin. Ten years before [*sic*], when the British star visited our theatre in Hollywood, she was the guest of the Brabins in their palatial Beverly Hills manor. A private motor car was at her disposal with her chauffeur. It was no Hollywood secret that the aging actress was without funds.
>
> Gossip columnists made much of the outrageous tantrums of the famous house-guest of the noted couple. My hostess dismissed it with a light wave of her hand. "Yes, Mr. Brock, there were times when Mrs. Campbell was, shall we put it, naughty? But I really didn't notice. You see, I knew her pain. The unending battle she had fought all her life…. Ah, what a supreme artist. I can still remember her glorious voice, her unrivaled beauty…"

Theda took her first airplane trip in 1935. The stewardess, K. Southworth of Redondo Beach, recalled Theda's first flight in a letter to Hedda Hopper in 1965:

> While checking passengers (all 14 of them) I came upon this astonishing woman. Black hair piled high, chalk white face pierced with those truly amazing eyes and covered from stem to stern, chin to knuckles by a black chiffon dress under this and enhanced by the shadowy fabric. She wore an armor of jewels and on the two inch window ledge near her were more, including a jeweled clock.
>
> I knew what would happen to those on the window when we hit the first down draft in Cajon Pass and who would be crawling under the seats finding them. So with some persuasion I got her to put them in her bag. There had been a death in her family and she was badly frightened and upset as this was also her first flight. My mention of "air bumps" only added to her apprehension.
>
> Togetherness being a fact of circumstance in a DC-2 in 1935 and my job being primarily to reassure passengers, I spent no little time with her. We talked of the inconsequential — but how I wanted to ask her about those unbelievable jewels — which she wore as easily as today's gals wear their pearls and basic black.
>
> She was dramatic, perhaps eccentric, but she stays in my mind, all other descriptions, fitting and otherwise aside, as a "fabulous being."

One old friend remembered that she — and Charles — could discuss at length things of general interest — not, he asserted, merely Beverly Hills society. "She knew world affairs, she knew music, they knew art. They were cultured people and the culture she had to get by herself."

In February 1939 Theda gave an account of a recent European trip with her husband to the *New York Journal*, which reported,

> They were in Rome when Hitler visited Mussolini and had two audiences with Pope Pius XI, and went through the Papal private apartments. "His Holiness didn't look his age," she said. "Through his death the world has lost a great friend." She was in London during the Munich crisis. "An official told me there would probably be an air raid within 3½ hours," she related. "I blurted out: 'won't they wait?' and everybody laughed at me." She thinks England is definitely a man's country. "Even the bathtubs are built for men," she said. "There is not even enough room in them for a woman's hips." Miss Bara also declared that the British press is muzzled and not free as in the U.S.

THIRTEEN.

Inactive but Not Forgotten

*D*uring World War II Hollywood, threw itself wholeheartedly into the war effort, just as it had done during the First World War. Studios such as Disney and directors such as Frank Capra (1897–1991) turned out propaganda films, actors such as Jimmy Stewart (1908–) actively went to war, entertainers such as Bob Hope (1903–) and Rita Hayworth (1918–1987) entertained the troops to keep up morale, estates were opened up for parties and many movie personalities worked and entertained in the Hollywood Canteen where lucky servicemen got a night off.

Theda Bara frequently worked in the Canteen, though most of the servicemen did not remember her or had only heard of her from an older generation. While she did not actually open up her home for parties for the servicemen, a former soldier told Hyman Belzberg, the owner of the house since 1982, that Charles had befriended him at the Canteen and brought him home to visit on several occasions.

In December 1949 Theda attended a party for about 50 Hollywood old-timers hosted by Cecil B. DeMille on the thirty-fifth anniversary of his first full-length movie, *The Squaw Man*. They drank punch, sized each other up, and were interviewed and photographed. *Time* magazine reported that others in attendance were Jack Holt (1888–1951), Francis X. Bushman and Mae Murray (1885–1965), who was pictured opposite Theda. One of the attendees, Ezra Goodman, recalled that Jesse Lasky (1880–1958), Mack Sennett (1884–1960), Ramon Novarro, Blanche Sweet and Winifred Kingston were also there. When *Time*'s cameraman suggested that the old-time male stars kneel in the front row for a group picture, Holt cracked, "If you get us old guys down on one knee, who's gonna get us up again?" Goodman recalled that Theda, now long past her vampire days, "was a rather shy, matronly figure at the party. 'What are you doing now?' I asked her. 'I'm keeping a very — I hope — happy home. Goodbye,' the ex-vamp replied as she scooted away."

Even after she became domestic there was a constant if small stream of genuine news or fan items about her, so she was never forgotten by those who had seen her on stage or screen. As the years rolled by she became a relic of the past and was occasionally sought out for her views as such. In 1929 *Screenland* ran a single page on "The Girl Who Made 'Theda' a Household Word"— and indeed it was. Among black college students in the 1950s and 1960s it was one of the ten most popular female names, all of which were rather exotic.

In 1932 when U.S. critics were asked to name the greatest all-time female star, Bara was third, behind Greta Garbo and Mary Pickford and ahead of Constance Bennett, Gloria Swanson and Marion Davies. At the same time *Screen Weekly* ran a full-page article about her in which Theda stressed the need for more glamour and mystery in the movies and declared that Garbo was the most glamorous; in 1934 she declared unequivocally that Garbo was "the supreme vampire of the screen ... if the essence of a successful vampire is to leave the audience convinced of the inevitability of the conquest." She also gave high marks to Marlene Dietrich, Katharine Hepburn and Mae West. Theda was habitually generous in making plugs for aspiring young actresses to Hedda Hopper and other film columnists, though she also panned a few.

In 1935-36 the Film Library of New York's Museum of Modern Art hit upon the idea of building up a visual history of the film industry since its inception 40 years earlier. As old films were gathered, they were shown to packed houses. In February 1936 *A Fool There Was* was shown. A reviewer gave her history and a recounting of the first Bara film, observing that "the public continued to cheer [but] the critics simply could not appreciate [her]," and concluded that "the vamp, as conceived by the early cinemas is dead. In 1936 Theda Bara is fascinating only because she's funny as she clutches at the shoulder strap of her nightie and purses her lips like an army post bugler."

By the 1930s she realized that she would never again be offered a starring role in an A grade picture. So she was probably willing to take lesser roles, perhaps good character parts. Unfortunately for her, since she had been out of pictures since 1926 she was known only as a silent star. By the 1930s the studios did not want to associate films with the silent stars because it dated the films. The public would suspect — with some justification — that it was probably a reissue of an older movie. Rather than being an asset, the name of a silent star might be a liability and might not even appear in the credits for that reason.

A famous example was *Noah's Ark*, made by Warner Bros. just prior to *The Jazz Singer*. Directed by Michael Curtiz, produced by Darryl Zanuck and made over the course of two years, it was released as a silent just as sound came to the movies. It was Warners' biggest loss; the male star, George O'Brien, later became a B cowboy actor for RKO and the female, cursed with a foreign but unsexy accent, never played again. Years later an independent company bought the film from Warners, added a sound track and narration, and successfully reissued it as

A striking photograph from the mid–1930s, when Bara was 50 (courtesy of the Academy of Motion Picture Arts and Sciences).

"Directed by Michael Curtiz and Produced by Darryl F. Zanuck." O'Brien, who was no longer acting, was not mentioned in the posters, but Curtiz (1888–1962) was an Academy Award–winning director and Zanuck (1902–1979), no longer with Warners, was a top Hollywood producer. Taking a lesson from that example, the studios viewed Theda's silent stardom as a strike against her.

In 1936 Paramount tempted her with a vamp role in *Hollywood Boulevard*,

which she didn't take. Then in 1939 she spoofed her former vamp character in
an appearance on the Ken Murray half of radio's *Texaco Hour*. Also in 1939
Darryl Zanuck completed a Technicolor history of the movies entitled *Hollywood Cavalcade*, recreating some of the outstanding events and personalities
of the old days. Naturally he included Theda's slinky, slithering vamp in a
sequence, using Lynn Bari (1915–) to play her.

In 1947 *Theatre Arts* magazine showed her among five actresses in a pictorial spread of "A Century of Cleopatras." *Harpers Bazaar* (1948) had a pictorial spread of "Living Legends" by Leo Lerman; there was Theda among over
a dozen notables such as statesman Alexander Kerensky, poet Edna St. Vincent Millay, Pola Negri and dancer Vaslav Nijinsky. Lerman commented,
"[Theda's] bizarre, libidinous movie pyrotechnics brought millions to Hollywood at the time of World War I; gave censors gray hair; raised her salary from
$160 to $4,000 a week; made her part of America's uninhibited mythology. She
was 'Queen of the Vamps.' Now she lives quietly with her ex-producer husband, Charles Brabin, in their Beverly Hills home."

She realized that her influence and fame were past and did not try to
trade on her old name but enjoyed latter-day recognition. The way in which
dentist Edward Furstman met her is indicative that her face, in the late 1940s,
was no longer instantly recognizable:

> I didn't know she was Theda Bara. She came in as Mrs. Brabin [in 1949].
> We were talking and I was taking her patient history and explaining the var-
> ious procedures and financial arrangements. She said "Fine," made an
> appointment for a later date and left. When she came back she mentioned
> that she had been in films. "You were?" I asked. "Did you go by the name of
> Brabin?" She said, "No, my actress name was Theda Bara." Just like that! I
> started. "My God, you're world famous." She started beaming as I continued,
> "I remember seeing you and I remember my mother and father talking about
> you, and my mother came in one time wearing one of those damned things
> with a feather in her hat. I thought she was trying to play an Indian, and my
> father asked, 'Who do you think you are, Theda Bara?'
>
> And she'd laugh like hell about that, thought it was very funny, because in
> the old days they used to wear this velvet thing around their head with an
> egret feather. And that's when I found out who she was. But it was always
> *Mrs. Brabin* though she appreciated the fact that I knew who she was and that
> I'd mentioned it to my office staff. They were just as surprised as I was.

As late as 1954 Alan Brock tried to interest Theda in a return to the stage
in a summer-stock tour. They discussed her silent screen career and then
began negotiating the stage comeback. Negotiations fell through because, as
she wrote to him in April, "I really don't think the few weeks in stock would
justify this long cross-country trip. I am quite sure that they would not pay
my transportation, would they? That alone would mean an outlay of at least

$500. The only thing that would interest me would be the tryout of a new Broadway possibility — and there is no suggestion of that in your present plan."

Though she was unable to return actively to films, the studios had not forgotten her. In February 1955 Columbia's Jerry Wald planned to use her as a technical adviser for a movie about her life, tentatively titled *The Great Vampire* and starring Betty Hutton (1921–) in the lead role. But other events interposed themselves and this was never to be.

FOURTEEN.
A "Notable Woman"

*T*he vamp of the '10s had become an old woman in the '50s. School-children on their way home used to pass the old woman and her husband as they tended their beloved rose garden at their home on Alpine. They stopped to talk to her, never realizing what she had meant to their grandparents. They thought of her as very friendly. Had they been a little older they would have noticed the elegance of her voice and bearing.

The voice, as a listener to the old Lux radio tape can hear, shows elocution training and reminds one of the elegance of Eleanor Roosevelt's upper New York state speech. Brock noted it as a British accent, which she explained as "not an affectation. The many years of living with Mr. Brabin, you know. After all my husband was born in England and spent much of his early life there. All of his friends, in and out of the picture industry are, of course, largely British.... And, I do so love fine speech."

The voice may have been affected by her teeth. Her dentist recalled that she had been given a bad set of dentures that "made her look like a goddamn horse," but that he gave her new ones, enabling her to smile, to eat comfortably and to be good-looking again.

Her handwriting was interesting. There was a definite Greek influence to it, the letter N being written as pi (π), for example, and E as epsilon (ε). She signed with a rubric, in the style of European aristocracy.

Maintaining her regal dignity, she always wore a veil when in public — though they were of pre–1940 style — and she was always well-dressed. Charles, as her consort, was also a sharp dresser, displaying good taste and style. She would not permit him to wear a tie or jacket with a single spot, so he was always meticulously attired. Theda's regal bearing was recalled in a typical incident by Bodeen:

> I remember once when she visited a Hollywood friend of mine for cock-tails. Her chauffeur brought her in the Brabin town car, and was instructed to call for her one hour hence. Promptly at five past the hour she peered at her diamond-studded wristwatch through her diamond-rimmed *lorgnette*

and said, "Theda Bara waits for no man." A taxi was called, and it arrived simultaneously with her chauffeur tardily at the wheel of her town car. Miss Bara brushed past the chauffeur without so much as a glance, got into the cab, and the town car followed the taxi to her home in Beverly Hills.

But some things could not be dismissed so imperiously. Cancer of the stomach is one of the most insidious and difficult cancers to diagnose because of a lack of specific symptoms. A gradual onset of indigestion in a person of previously good health with symptoms suggesting a peptic ulcer develops into anemia, unexplained weight loss and loss of appetite before the cancer goes on to kill. In the 1950s and 1960s, radical surgery could help only about one in five of its victims.

In 1954, while she was negotiating for a summer stock comeback with Brock, Theda Bara underwent four operations for stomach cancer. On February 13, 1955, just after Columbia bought the rights to her life story, she entered California Lutheran Hospital in Los Angeles with the uncured cancer. Six weeks later she lapsed into a coma from which she never regained consciousness, and early in the evening of Thursday, April 7, 1955, she died alone, although Charles and Lori were daily visitors.

The next day newspapers throughout the world carried the story, and if she ever thought she was forgotten, front-page stories in many papers belied that notion. The *Los Angeles Times* headlined "First Femme Fatale of Movies Loses Her Fight Against Cancer"; the *Los Angeles Herald-Examiner,* writing "The Vamp is dead," called her "a gracious and beautiful Hollywood pioneer who drove envious housewives hysterical and their husbands into a trance." The *Oakland Tribune* ran four portraits of "The" Vampire. Other papers carried the Associated Press account of her life, career and death. *Variety* announced her death on the 13th, *Time* magazine reported it on the 18th and across the sea, the *London Times* announced "with regret the death of Miss Theda Bara, a star of the silent films."

Her hometown paper, the *Cincinnati Enquirer*, editorialized on the 11th; "To our [generation] she was a vicarious thrill of majestic proportions." And the *New York Times* editorialized as follows on the 9th:

> Her audiences loved her, the men because of her unmixed femininity, the women because they were sympathetically concerned with the technique.... On the silent screen she appealed to men's most primitive instincts. On the screen she was, indeed, a bad girl, and this was her allure. Off the screen she was a good woman, happily married for 34 years.... Many among us who are close to her age, or even younger, will think warm and grateful thoughts of her, now that she is gone. She took other people's minds off their troubles: is not this a tribute worth having?

On a personal level her dentist noted, "Everyone I ever knew remembered her fondly. Never had a bad word to say about her."

Her funeral was arranged by Pierce Brothers Beverly Hills Mortuary for April 9, the day before Easter. Her body was cremated and the ashes were placed in the Columbarium of Memory at Forest Lawn, Glendale, behind a simple plaque bearing only the words "Theda Bara Brabin   1955."

On April 18, her will to an estate of over $100,000 was filed. Her brother had died before her and his widow, Alma M. Bara of Newport, Rhode Island, received $1,000. Theda's still-living mother was not mentioned. Her sister received the bulk of the estate and the Motion Picture Relief Fund, which provides a convalescent and retirement home for film stars, received most of what was left. Charles, who was independently wealthy, was bequeathed $800 and her engagement and wedding rings "as a remembrance of our happy marriage." A friend recalled that whenever he saw Charles after Theda's death, he appeared devastated by his loss.

Her mother died in July 1957 at the home she shared with Lori in Westwood, Charles died in a hospital in Santa Monica in November 1957, and Lori moved to Marycrest Manor, a Catholic residence home in Culver City where she lived until her death in August 1965.

At Marycrest Lori converted to Catholicism. Nurse Diane Kisro remembered that she would "knock herself out to get dressed, to look perfect, even though she could hardly move with that cigarette-caused emphysema." She also remembered that Lori was very friendly, both to her and to her two small sons. She loved to have visitors and helped Marycrest hire its first pharmacist by actively seeking him out. Lori was affluent but in later years complained that she was forced to live on her principal, having run through her interest. Lori left half of her $400,000 estate to the Motion Picture Relief Fund in Theda's name, $100,000 to Marycrest, and most of the remaining quarter to various children's hospitals.

In August 1957 Charles auctioned off Theda's jewelry collection in Chicago, where she had had many friends in the days when it was a movie center. The collection featured diamonds up to seven carats and delicately designed diamond, emerald and platinum pieces. In 1961 her name made a small splash in the film trade papers when Warner Brothers used her 1927 Rolls-Royce for its period gangster movie *Portrait of a Mobster*. Of her many films only the first and last — *A Fool There Was* and *Madame Mystery* — survive intact. Bits and pieces of others survive, but the rest have been lost to decomposition over the years.

Why Jerry Wald's 1955 plans to film her life story for Columbia never went anywhere is a puzzle. Perhaps the answer lies in Columbia's experience with biographies. The studio had a good deal of luck with some biographies, and the Al Jolson story was one of its most successful films. Its Valentino biography, however, was a failure. Since Valentino's name was much bigger than Bara's, the studio probably decided the project was too great a risk. If such a movie ever materializes, it is to be hoped that it will be a serious biography such as the ones Universal did for Lon Chaney, Rod Steiger did for W. C. Fields and Robert Downey, Jr., did for Chaplin. To play it for laughs, like Betty Hutton's travesty on Pearl White, would, as the silent screen historian Joe Franklin observed, "do a disservice not only to the industry and the cause of film history, but to the memory of a great performer as well."

Many of the silent stars have today slipped into oblivion, their memory eroding from public consciousness even as their films disintegrate with age. But no oblivion for Theda Bara. In 1986 the California Historical Society, looking back over two centuries, listed her as one of 88 California women among those included in *Notable American Women*. In April 1994 the U.S. Postal Service commemorated her along with nine other silent stars with a commemorative stamp. College-educated vamp, "feminist" by her own account, contented wife, movie star, serious actress, writer, and international social butterfly she certainly deserves the honors of being called "notable" and of gracing a stamp four decades after her death. She would have liked that.

Stage and Screen Appearances

The Devil (play, New York with the Edwin Stevens Company, August 18, 1908).

Cast: Edwin Stevens (The Devil [Dr Miller]); Dorothy Dorr (Olga Hoffmann); Frank Monroe (Herman Hoffmann); Marguerite Snow (Elsa Berg); Theodosia de Coppet (Mme. Schleswig); Henry Clark (Herr Grosser); Tiny Marshall (Mme. Lassen); Paul McAllister (Karl Mahler); Marion Lorine (Naomi); Nan Lewald (Mme. Zanden); Jane Murray (Mme. Reineke); W. Chrystie Miller (Heinrich); Arthur Hoyt (Herr Besser); Franklin Bixby (Manservant).

Staged by Robert Milton. Settings by Walter Burridge. Adapted from Ferenc Molnar by Oliver Herford. Produced by Henry Savage.

The Quaker Girl (play, New Orleans with the #2 Company, 1912).

Written by James Tanner. Lyrics by Adrian Ross and Percy Greenbank. Music by Lionel Monckton.

Just Like John (play, on the road, August 12, 1912). Cast: Walter Jones (John Endicott); Helene Lackaye (His wife).

Written by George Broadhurst and Mark Swan. Adapted by M. E. Swan.

A Fool There Was (Fox; 6 reels; filmed 1914; released January 1915).

Cast: Theda Bara (The Vampire); Edward José (John Schuyler); Mabel Fremyer (Kate Schuyler); Kate Allison (Her sister); Clifford Bruce (Friend of the Schuylers); Victor Benoit (Victim of the Vampire, Parmalee); Frank Powell (The Doctor); Minna Gale (The doctor's fiancée); Runa Hodges (The child); Creighton Hale.

Written by Porter Emerson Brown. Photographed by Roy L. Caldwell. Directed by Frank Powell.

Sources: *New York Telegraph*, January 18, 1929; *New York Times*, March 16, 1920; The American Film Institute *Catalog of Motion Pictures Produced in the United States: Feature Films, 1911–1920* and second volume, *Feature Films, 1921–1930*; *Oakland Tribune*, June 8, 1931; *LA Times*, May 24, 1934; Bodeen, *From Hollywood*, pp. 25–28; the Billy Rose Theatre Collection of the New York Public Library.

The Kreutzer Sonata (Fox; 5309 feet; released March 1915).

Cast: Theda Bara (Esther Rusoff/ Celia Friedlander); Nance O'Neil (Miriam Friedlander); William E. Shay (Gregor Randar); Mimi Yvonne; Jacob Gordon.

Directed and written by Herbert Brenon (from Jacob Gordon's version of Tolstoy's play). Bara's billing: "The Woman of 1000 Faces."

The Clemenceau Case (Fox; 6 reels; in Britain called *Infidelity*; released April 1915).

Cast: Theda Bara (Iza Dobromowska); William E. Shay (Pierre Clemenceau); Stuart Holmes (Constantin Ritz); Jane Lee (Janet); Mrs. Cecil Raleigh (Countess Dobromowska); Frank Goldsmith (Duke Sergius); Mrs. Allen Walker (Marie Clemenceau); Sidney Shields (Mme. Ritz).

Directed and written by Herbert Brenon (from a play by Martha Woodrow from a novel by Alexandre Dumas, *fils*). Photography by Philip Rosen. Bara's billing: first time as a star, with her name in large letters above the title.

The Devil's Daughter (Fox; 5 reels; 4800 feet; working title *The Vampire*; released June 1915).

Cast: Theda Bara (Gioconda Dianti); Paul Doucet (Lucio Settala); Victor Benoit (Cosimo Dalbo); Robert Wayne (Lorenzo Gaddi); Jane Lee (Little Beata); Doris Heywood (Silvia Settala); Jane Miller (Francesca Doni); Elaine Ivans (La Sirenetta); Clifford Bruce; Edouard Durand (Roffiano).

Directed and written by Frank Powell (from Gabriele D'Annunzio's play *La gioconda*, as translated by Joseph Trant and adapted by Garfield Thompson. Photography by David Calcagni.

Lady Audley's Secret (Fox; 5 reels; 5000 feet; in Britain called *Secrets of Society*; released August 1915).

Cast: Theda Bara (Lady Audley); Clifford Bruce; William Riley Hatch (Luke Martin); Stephen Gratten; Warner Richmond.

Directed by Marshall Farnum. Written by Mary Asquith (from novel and play of Miss M. E. Braddon). Photography by Norton Davis. Theda's billing: "The most wickedly beautiful face in the entire world."

The Two Orphans (Fox; 5–7 reels; 5374 feet; working title *The Hunchback*; released September 1915).

Cast: Theda Bara (Henriette); Jean Southern (Louise); William E. Shay (The Chevalier de Vaudrey); Herbert Brenon (Pierre); Gertrude Berkley (Mother Frochard); Frank Goldsmith (Marquis de Presles); E. L. Fernandez (Jacques); Sheridan Block (Count de Liniere); Mrs. Cecil Raleigh (Countess de Liniere); John Daly Murphy (Picard).

Directed and written by Herbert Brenon (from the play by Adolphe D'Ennery). Photography by Philip Rosen.

Sin (Fox; 5 reels; working title *The Jewels of the Madonna*; released October 1915).

Cast: Theda Bara (Rosa [as listed in *Variety*; Bodeen lists the character as

Cora]); Warner Oland (Pietro); William E. Shay (Luigi); Louise Rial (Maria); Henry Leone (Giovanni).

Directed and written by Herbert Brenon (from a story by Nixola Daniels). Photography by Philip Rosen. Theda's billing: "Destiny's Dark Angel."

Carmen (Fox; 5 reels; released November 1915).

Cast: Theda Bara (Carmen); Einar Linden (José); Elsie MacLeod (Michaela); Carl Harbaugh (Escamillo); J.A. Marcus (Dancaire); E. de Varny (Captain Morales); Fay Tunis (Carlotta); Joseph P. Green.

Directed and written by Raoul Walsh (from the novel by Prosper Mérimée). Photography by Georges Benoit and George Schneiderman.

The Galley Slave (Fox; 5 reels, 4859 feet; released November 1915).

Cast: Theda Bara (Frances Brabaut); Claire Whitney (Cecily Blaine); Lillian Lawrence (Mrs. Blaine); Ben Hendricks (Mr. Blaine); Stuart Holmes (Antoine Brabaut); Jane Lee (Dolores); Hardee Kirkland (Baron de Bois); Henry Leone; A. H. Van Buren.

Directed by J. Gordon Edwards. Written by Clara Beranger (from Rex Ingram's adaptation of Bartley Campbell's play). Theda's billing: "Destiny's Dark Angel."

Destruction (Fox; 5 reels; released December 1915).

Cast: Theda Bara (Ferdinande); J. Herbert Frank (Dave Walker); James Furey (John Froment); Gaston Bell (John Froment III); Warner Oland (Mr. Deleveau); Esther Hoier (Josine Walker); Master Tansey (Josine's brother); Arthur Morrison (Lang); Frank Evans (Mill foreman); Carleton Macy.

Directed and written by Will Davis (from his own story, "Labor"). Bara's billing: "The most famous vampire in her most daring role brings ruin and disaster to thousands."

The Serpent (Fox; 6 reels; in Britain *Fires of Hate*; released January 1916).

Cast: Theda Bara (Vania Lazar); James Marcus (Ivan Lazar); Lillian Hathaway (Martsa Lazar); Charles Craig (Grand Duke Valanoff); Carl Harbaugh (Prince Valanoff); George Walsh (Andrey Sobi); Nan Carter (Ema Lachno); Marcel Morhange (Gregoire).

Directed and written by Raoul Walsh, with assistance in writing from George Walsh (from Philip Bartholomae's story, "The Wolf's Claw"). Photography by George Benoit.

Gold and the Woman (Fox; 6 reels; working title *Retribution;* released March 1916).

Cast: Theda Bara (Juliet DeCordova [as listed in *Variety*; Bodeen gives the character of Theresa DeCordova]); Alma Hanlon (Hester Gray); H. Cooper Cliffe (Col. Ernest Dent); Harry Hilliard (Lee Duskara); Carleton Macy (Dugald Chandes); Chief Black Eagle (Chief Duskara); Julia Hurley (Duskara's squaw); Carter Harkness (Leelo Duskara); Caroline Harris; Ted Griffin; Louis Stern; James Sheehan; Frank Whitson; Pauline Barry.

Directed by James Vincent. Written by Mary Murillo (from a story by Daniel Roosevelt).

The Eternal Sapho (Fox; 5 reels; in Britain, *Bohemia*; released May 1916).
   Cast: Theda Bara (Laura Grubbins [as listed in *Variety*; Bodeen lists the character as Moya Wilson, model]); James Cooley (Billy Malvern); Walter Lewis (Mr. Marvern, Sr); Harriet Delaro (Mrs. Marvern, Sr); Einar Linden (John Drummond); Mary Martin (Mrs. Drummond); Kittens Reichert (Their child); George MacQuarrie (Jack McCullogh); Warner Oland (H. Coudal); Frank Norcross (Grubbins); Caroline Harris (Mother Grubbins).
   Directed by Bertram Bracken. Written by Mary Murillo (from Daudet's novel *Sapho*). Photography by Rial Schellinger.

East Lynne (Fox; 5 reels; 5600 feet; released June 1916).
   Cast: Theda Bara (Lady Isabel Carlisle); Stuart Holmes (Captain Levison); William Tooker (Her father); Claire Whitney (Barbara Hare); Stanhope Wheatcroft; Eugenie Woodward; Ben Deeley (Archibald Carlisle); James O'Connor; Emily Fitzroy; Eldean Stewart (The Carlisle son); Loel Stewart (The Carlisle daughter); Velma Whitman; H. Evans; Eugenie Woodward; Frank Norcross; Ethel Fleming.
   Directed by Bertram Bracken. Written by Mary Murillo (from Mary Elizabeth Braddon's play of Ellen Wood's novel). Photography by Rial Schellinger.

Under Two Flags (Fox; 6 reels; released July 1916).
   Cast: Theda Bara (Cigarette); Herbert Heyes (Bertie Cecil); Stuart Holmes (Chateauroye); Stanhope Wheatcroft (Berkley Cecil); Joseph Crehan (Rake); Charles Craig (Rockingham); Claire Whitney (Venetia).
   Directed by J. Gordon Edwards. Written by George Hall (from Ouida's novel). Photography by Philip Rosen.

Her Double Life (Fox; 6 reels; released September 1916).
   Cast: Theda Bara (Mary Doone); Stuart Holmes (Lloyd Stanley); Walter Law (Mary's foster father); Lucia Moore; Jane Lee; A. H. Van Buren (Elliott Clifford); Madeleine Le Nard (Ethel Wardley); Katherine Lee (Mary as a little girl); Carey Lee.
   Directed by J. Gordon Edwards. Written by Mary Murillo (from her story, "The New Magdalen"). Photography by Philip Rosen.

Romeo and Juliet (Fox; 7 reels; released October 1916).
   Cast: Theda Bara (Juliet); Harry Hilliard (Romeo); Glen White (Mercutio); Walter Law (Friar Lawrence); John Webb Dillion (Tybalt); Einar Linden (Paris); Elwin Eaton (Montague); Alice Gale (Nurse); Helen Tracy (Lady Capulet); Victory Bateman (Lady Montague); Edwin Holt (Capulet); Jane Lee; Katherine Lee; May DeLacy.
   Directed by J. Gordon Edwards. Written by Adrian Johnson (from the play by William Shakespeare). Photography by Phil Rosen. Cutting by Alfred De Gaetano.

The Vixen (Fox; 6 reels; in Britain, *The Love Pirate*; released December 1916).

Cast: Theda Bara (Elsie Drummond); A. H. Van Buren (Martin Stevens); Herbert Heyes (Knowles Murray); Mary Martin (Helen Drummond); George Clarke (Admiral Drummond); Carl Gerard (Charlie Drummond); George Odell (Butler).

Directed by J. Gordon Edwards. Written by Mary Murillo. Photography by Philip Rosen.

The Darling of Paris (Fox; 6 reels; released January 1917).

Cast: Theda Bara (Esmeralda); Glen White (Quasimodo); Walter Law (Claude Frallo); Herbert Heyes (Captain Phoebus); Carey Lee (Paquette); Alice Gale (Gypsy Queen); John Webb Dillion (Clopin); Louis Dean (Gringouire).

Directed by J. Gordon Edwards. Written by Adrian Johnson (from Hugo's *Hunchback of Notre Dame*. Photography by Philip Rosen.

The Tiger Woman (Fox; 6 reels; in Britain, *Behind a Throne*; released February 1917).

Cast: Theda Bara (Countess Irma, later Princess Petrovich); E. F. Roseman (Prince Petrovich); Louis Dean (The Baron); Emil DeVarney (The Count); John Webb Dillion (Stevan); Glen White (Edwin Harris); Mary Martin (Mrs. Edwin Harris); Herbert Heyes (Mark Harris); Kittens Reichert (Their child); Edwin Holt (Harris boy's father); Florence Martin (Marion Harding); George Clarke (Marion's father); Kate Blancke (Marion's mother).

Directed by J. Gordon Edwards. Written by Adrian Johnson (from a story by James Adams). Photography by Philip Rosen. Bara's billing: "The Champion Vampire of the Season."

Her Greatest Love (Fox; 5 reels; in Britain, *Redemption*; released April 1917).

Cast: Theda Bara (Vera Herbert [as listed in *Variety*; Bodeen lists the character as Hazel]); Marie Curtis (Lady Dolly); Walter Law (Prince Zuroff); Glen White (Lord Jura); Harry Hilliard (Lucien Correze); Callie Torres (Jeanne de Sonnaz); Alice Gale (Old nurse); Grace Saum (Maid).

Directed by J. Gordon Edwards. Written by Adrian Johnson (from Ouida's *Moths*). Photography by Philip Rosen.

Heart and Soul (Fox; 5 reels; released May 1917).

Cast: Theda Bara (Jess); Edwin Holt (Middle-aged planter); Claire Whitney (Bess); Walter Law (Drummond); Harry Hilliard (John Neil); Glen White (Pedro); John Webb Dillion (Sancho); Alice Gale (Mammy); Margaret Laird; Kittens Reichert.

Directed by J. Gordon Edwards. Written by Adrian Johnson (from Haggard's novel). Photography by Philip Rosen.

Camille (Fox; 6 reels; released September 1917).

Cast: Theda Bara (Camille); Albert Roscoe (Armand Duval); Walter Law (Count de Varville); Alice Gale (Madame Prudence); Glen White (Gaston Rieux); Claire Whitney (Celeste).

Directed by J. Gordon Edwards. Written by Adrian Johnson (from the novel and play by Dumas, *fils*). Photography by Rial Schellinger. Bara's billing: "A Masterpiece of the Bara Art — A Theda Bara Super Picture."

Cleopatra (Fox; 11 reels; released October 1917).
Cast: Theda Bara (Cleopatra); Fritz Leiber (Caesar); Thurston Hall (Antony); Henri deVries (Octavius); Art Acord (Kephren); Albert Roscoe (Pharon); Genevieve Blinn; Dorothy Drake (Charmian); Dell Duncan (Iras); Hector V. Sarno (Messenger); Herschel Mayall (Ventidius).
Directed by J. Gordon Edwards. Written by Adrian Johnson (from Shakespeare and Sardou).

The Rose of Blood (Fox; 7 reels; released November 1917).
Cast: Theda Bara (Lisza Tapenka); Richard Ordynski (Vassya); Charles Clary (Prince Arbassoff); Herschel Mayall (Koliensky); Marie Kiernan (Kostya); Bert Turner; Genevieve Blinn (Governess); Joe King; Hector Sarno (Revolutionary).
Directed by J. Gordon Edwards. Written by Bernard McConville (from Ordyniski's story *The Red Rose*). Photography by Rial Schellinger and John Boyle.

Madame Du Barry (Fox; 7 reels; released December 1917).
Cast: Theda Bara (Madame Du Barry); Charles Clary (Louis XV); Herschel Mayall (Jean Du Barry); Fred Church (Cossé-Brissac); Genevieve Blinn (Duchess de Gaumont); Willard Louis (Guillaume Du Barry); Hector Sarno (Lebel); Dorothy Drake (Henriette); Rosita Marstini (Mother Savord); Joe King; James Conley; A. Fremont.
Directed by J. Gordon Edwards. Written by Adrian Johnson (from a Dumas, *père* novel). Photography by Rial Schellinger and John Boyle.

The Forbidden Path (Fox; 6 reels; released February 1918).
Cast: Theda Bara (Mary Lynde); Hugh Thompson (Robert Sinclair); Sidney Mason (Felix Benavente); Walter Law (Mr. Lynde); Florence Martin (Barbara Reynolds); Wynne Hope Allen (Mrs. Lynde); Alphonse Ethier (William Sinclair); Lisle Leigh (Mrs. Bryne); Reba Porter (Tessie Bryne).
Directed by J. Gordon Edwards. Written by E. Lloyd Sheldon (from his story *From the Depths*). Photography by John Boyle.

The Soul of Buddha (Fox; 5 reels; released April 1918).
Cast: Theda Bara (Bava); Hugh Thompson (Sir John Dare); Victor Kennard (Ysora); Anthony Merlo (Count Romaine); Florence Martin (The count's wife); Jack Ridgeway (Her father); Henry Warwick (Stage manager).
Directed by J. Gordon Edwards. Written by Adrian Johnson (from a story by Theda Bara). Photography by John Boyle.

Under the Yoke (Fox; 5 reels; released June 1918).
Cast: Theda Bara (Maria Valverde); Albert Roscoe (Captain Paul Winter); G. Raymond Nye (Diablo Ramirez); E.B. Tilton (Don Ramon Valverde); Carrie Clark Ward (The duenna).

Directed by J. Gordon Edwards. Written by Adrian Johnson (from a George Scarborough story, *Maria of the Roses*). Photography by John Boyle and Harry Gerstad. Advertised as "A volcanic drama of the Philippines — She scorched her soul to save an American cavalry officer."

Salome (Fox; 8 reels; released August 1918).
Cast: Theda Bara (Salome); G. Raymond Nye (Herod); Albert Roscoe (John the Baptist); Bertram Grassby (Prince David); Herbert Heyes (Sejanus); Genevieve Blinn (Queen Miriam); Vera Doria (Naomi); Alfred Fremont (Galba).
Directed by J. Gordon Edwards. Written by Adrian Johnson (from Flavius Josephus' chronicles). Photography by John Boyle. Music by George Rubenstein.

When a Woman Sins (Fox; 7 reels; released September 1918).
Cast: Theda Bara (Lillian Marchand/Poppea); Joseph Swickard (Mortimer West); Albert Roscoe (Michael West); Alfred Fremont (Augustus Van Brooks); Jack Rollens (Reggie West); Genevieve Blinn (Mrs West); Ogden Crane (Dr Stone).
Directed by J. Gordon Edwards. Written by E. Lloyd Sheldon (from Betta Breuil's story *The Message of the Lillies*). Photography by John Boyle. Advertised as "The Greatest Woman's Story ever told — the regeneration of a modern Vampire."

The She-Devil (Fox; 6 reels; released December 1918).
Cast: Theda Bara (Lolette); Albert Roscoe (Maurice Tabor); Frederick Bond (Apollo); George A. McDaniel (The Tiger).
Directed by J. Gordon Edwards. Written by George Neje Hopkins ("Neje"). Photography by John Boyle and Harry Gerstad. Advertised as "The story of a woman who raised havoc with a dozen lovers."

The Light (Fox; 5 reels; released January 1919).
Cast: Theda Bara (Blanchette Dumonde); Eugene Ormonde (Chabin); Robert Walker (Etienne Desechette); George Renevant (Auchat); Florence Martin (Jeanette).
Directed by J. Gordon Edwards. Written by Adrian Johnson and Charles Kenyon (from Luther Reed and Brett Page).

When Men Desire (Fox; 5 reels; released March 1919).
Cast: Theda Bara (Marie Lohr); Flemming Ward (Robert Stedman); G. Raymond Nye (Major Wolf Von Rohn); Florence Martin (Elsie Henner); Maude Hill (Lola Santez); Edward Elkus (Professor Lohr).
Directed by J. Gordon Edwards. Written by Adrian Johnson (from E. Lloyd Sheldon and J. Searle Dawley, *The Scarlet Altars*). Photography by John Boyle. Advertised as "Womanhood Outraged — the thrilling adventures of a woman who tried to be true."

The Siren's Song (Fox; 5 reels; released May 1919).

Cast: Theda Bara (Marie Bernais/Marinelli); Alfred Fremont (Jules Bernais); Ruth Handforth (Aunt Caroline); L. C. Shumway (Raoul Nieppe); Albert Roscoe (Gaspard Prevost); Paul Weigel (Hector Remey); Carrie Clark Ward (Paulette Remey).

Directed by J. Gordon Edwards. Written by Charles Kenyon. Photography by John Boyle.

A Woman There Was (Fox; 5 reels; released June 1919).

Cast: Theda Bara (Zara); Winthrop Davidson (listed in *Variety* as Winthrop; some other sources list him as William) (Rev. Charles Stark); Robert Elliott (Pulke); Claude Payton (High Priest); John Ardizoni (Majah).

Directed by J. Gordon Edwards. Written by Adrian Johnson (from a Neje story, *Creation's Tears*). Photography by John Boyle.

La Belle Russe (Fox; 5 reels; released September 1919).

Cast: Theda Bara (twin sisters: Fleurette and "La Belle Russe"); Warburton Gamble (Philip Sackton); Marian Stewart (Philip Sackton, Jr); Robert Lee Keeling (Sir James Sackton); William B. Davidson (Brand); Alice Wilson (Lady Sackton); Robert Vivian (Butler); Lewis Broughton.

Directed and written by Charles Brabin (from a David Belasco play). Photography by George Lane.

Kathleen Mavourneen (Fox; 6 reels; copyrighted August 1919; released October 1919).

Cast: Theda Bara (Kathleen Mavourneen); Edward O'Connor (Kathleen's father); Jennie Dickerson (Kathleen's mother); Raymond McKee (Terence O'Moore); Marc McDermott (The Squire of Tralee); Marica Harris (Lady Clancarthy); Henry Hallam (Sir John Clancarthy); Harry Gripp (Dennis O'Rourke); Morgan Thorpe (Father O'Flynn).

Directed and written by Charles Brabin (from Tom Moore's poem and Dion Boucicault's play). Titles and Inserts photography by Richard Maedler. Advertised as "The Sweetest Irish love story ever told."

The Lure of Ambition (Fox; 5 reels; released November 1919).

Cast: Theda Bara (Olga Dolan); Thurlow Bergen (Duke of Rutledge); William B. Davidson (Hon. Cyril Ralston); Dan Mason (Sylvester Dolan); Ida Waterman (The duchess); Amelia Gardner (Lady Constance); Robert Patton Gibbs (Miguel Lopez); Dorothy Drake (Muriel Ralston); Peggy Parr (Minnie Dolan); Tammany Young (Dan Hicks).

Directed and written by Edmund Lawrence (from a Julia Burnham story). Photography by Alderson Leach. Titles and Insert photography by Richard Maedler.

The Blue Flame (play, New York with the A. H. Wood Company, March 15, 1920.

Cast: Alan Dinehart (John Varnum); Jack Gibson (Ah Foo); Donald Gallaher (Larry Winston); Helen Curry (Cicely Varnum); Kenneth Hill (Ned Maddox);

Thais Lawton (Clarissa Archibald); Theda Bara (Ruth Gordon); Earl House (The stranger); Tessie Lawrence (Nora Macrew); Harry Mintura (Tom Dorgan); Tom O'Hara (Miller); Frank Hughes (Patterson); DeWitt C. Jennings (Inspector Ryan); Henry Herbert (Quong Toy); Joseph Buckley (Barnes); Martin Malloy (Groggins); Robert Lee (Wung Ming); Royal Stout (Ling Foo).

Written by: George Hobart and John Willard (from a play by Lois N. Vance). Produced by A. H. Woods. Directed by J.C. Huffman and W. H. Gilmore.

The Unchastened Woman (Chadwick, 7 reels; released October 1925).

Cast: Theda Bara (Caroline Knollys); Wyndham Standing (Hubert Knollys); Dale Fuller (Hildegarde Sanbury); John Miljan (Lawrence Sanbury); Harry Northrup (Michael Krellen); Eileen Percy (Emily Madden); Mayme Kelso (Susan Ambie).

Directed by James Young. Written by Douglas Doty (from a play by Louis Anspacher). Photography by William O'Connell.

Madame Mystery (Hal Roach-Pathé; 2 reels; released December 1926).

Cast: Theda Bara ("Madame Mystery"); James Finlayson; Tyler Brooke; "Babe" (Oliver) Hardy; Fred Malatesta.

Directed by Richard Wallace and Stan Laurel. Written by Hal Roach.

The Red Devil (playlet for vaudeville, New York, January 18, 1929).

Cast: Theda Bara; Al Herman.

Written by Theda Bara.

Fata Morgana (play Oakland, CA, with the Elsie Ferguson Company, June 7, 1931).

Cast: Jack Thomas (George); Norman Field (Mr. Fay); Theda Bara (Mrs. Fay); Mattie Hyde (George's mother).

Produced by Elsie Ferguson. Adapted from Ernest Vajda by Elsie Ferguson.

Bella Donna (play, Beverly Hills Little Theater, May 21, 1934).

Cast: John T. Murray (Dr. Isaacson); Walter Armitage (Baroudi); Ramsey Hill (Nigel); Arthur Loft (The young doctor); Theda Bara (Bella Donna).

Directed by Monty Collins. Sets by Nuncie Sabina Bittman. Adapted from Robert Hichens by James Fagan.

Bibliography

The Theda Bara File at the Film Library of the Academy of Motion Picture Arts and Sciences contains many unsigned, undated or unattributed items relating to Theda Bara. The same library's Hedda Hopper File includes three letters, two from Bara to Hopper and one from Hopper to Bara. The library also holds a tape of *Lux Radio Theatre* (June 8, 1936), on which Bara appeared. Items have been listed as thoroughly as possible; however, many are from clippings files in libraries and at the newspapers or magazines themselves, so complete information was not available.

BOOKS

Adams, James, ed. *Album of American History* (New York: Scribners, 1948), IV, p. 357.

Allen, Frederick. *Only Yesterday* (New York: Harper's, 1931), p. 10.

American Film Institute Staff. *The American Film Institute Catalog of Motion Pictures Produced in the United States: Feature Films, 1911–1920* (Berkeley: University of California Press, 1988), 2 vols.

_____. *The American Film Institute Catalog of Motion Pictures Produced in the United States: Feature Films, 1921–1930* (Berkeley: University of California Press, 1991).

Auriol, G. A., et al. *Le Cinéma: Des Origines à Nos Jours* (Paris: Cygne, 1932), p. 211.

Birmingham, Stephen. *The Rest of Us* (New York: Berkeley, 1984), pp. 189, 192.

Blesh, Rudi. *Keaton* (New York: Macmillan, 1966), pp. 125, 128.

Bodeen, DeWitt. *From Hollywood...* (New York: Barnes, 1976), pp. 13–28.

Bowan, Lynn. *Los Angeles* (Berkeley: Howell-North, 1974), ch. 7.

Bronner, Edwin. *The Encyclopedia of American Theatre, 1900–1975* (San Diego: Barnes, 1980), p. 58.

Brown, Curtis. *Jean Harlow* (New York: Pyramid, 1977), p. 60.

Cary, Diana. *Hollywood's Children* (Boston: Houghton-Mifflin, 1979), p. 165.

Condit, Carl. *The Railroad and the City* (Columbus: Ohio State University Press, 1977), p. 109.

Conners, Marilyn. *What Chance Have I in Hollywood?* (Hollywood: Famous Authors, 1924), p. 53.

Cooper, Miriam. *Dark Lady of the Silents* (New York: Bobbs-Merrill, 1973), pp. 101, 103, 116–118, 165, 197.

DeMille, Cecil B. *The Autobiography of Cecil B. DeMille*, ed. Donald Hayne (Englewood Cliffs, NJ: Prentice-Hall, 1959), p. 64.

Eames, John D. *The MGM Story* (New York: Crown, 1976), pp. 8, 18, 57, 60, 72, 76, 80, 82, 84, 85, 86, 95, 97, 102.

Florescu, Radu, and McNally, Raymond. *Dracula: A Biography of Vlad the Impaler*, (New York: Hawthorne, 1973), pp. 173, 174.

Florey, Robert. *Filmland* (Paris: Cinémagazine, 1923), p. 276.

____. *Hollywood Années Zero* (Paris: Seghers, 1972), pp. 69, 128, 129, 132.

Ford, Charles. *La Vie Quotidienne à Hollywood (1915–35)* (Paris: Hachette, 1972), p. 52.

Franklin, Joe. *Classics of the Silent Screen* (New York: Bramhall, 1959), p. 125.

Gabor, Mark. *The Pin-Up* (New York: Universe, 1973), pp. 108, 110.

Gehring, Wes. *W.C. Fields: A Bio-Bibliography* (Westport, CT: Greenwood, 1984), pp. 15, 16.

Gish, Lillian. *Lillian Gish: The Movies, Mr. Griffith and Me* (Englewood Cliffs, NJ: Prentice-Hall, 1969), p. 167.

Glut, Donald. *The Dracula Book* (Metuchen, NJ: Scarecrow, 1975), pp. 21, 25, 45.

Goodman, Ezra. *The Fifty Year Decline and Fall of Hollywood* (New York: Simon & Schuster, 1961), pp. 26, 327, 365, 368, 377.

Graham, Sheila. *The Garden of Allah* (New York: Crown, 1970), pp. 18, 37.

Griffith, Richard and Mayer, Arthur. *The Movies* rev. ed. (New York: Simon & Schuster, 1970), pp. 66–69.

Halliwell, Leslie. *The Filmgoer's Companion.* 6th ed. (New York: Hill & Wang, 1977).

Hampton, Benjamin Boles. *A History of the Movies* (1931; reprint New York: Arno, 1970), pp. 88, 219–220, 335–336.

Hart, James D. *A Companion to California* (New York: Oxford, 1977).

Havighurst, Walter. *Ohio: A Bicentennial History* (New York: Norton, 1976), pp. 74–76.

Heller, Murray. ed. *Black Names in America: Origins and Usage* (Cleveland: Cleveland Public Library, 1975), p. 521.

Henstell, Bruce. *Sunshine and Wealth: Los Angeles in the 20s and 30s* (San Francisco: Chronicle, 1984), p. 80.

Katz, Ephraim. *The Film Encyclopedia* (New York: Crowell, 1979).

Kerr, Walter. *The Silent Clowns* (New York: Knopf, 1975), pp. 114, 320.

Kobal, John, ed. *50 Years of Movie Posters* (New York: Bounty, nd), pp. 17, 20.

____. *Hollywood: The Years of Innocence* (London: Thames, 1985), pp. 30, 129, 133–134.

Kobler, John. *Damned in Paradise: The Life of John Barrymore* (New York: Atheneum, 1977), p. 271.

Lahue, Kalton. *Ladies in Distress* (New York: Barnes, 1971), pp. 19–29.

LeRoy, Mervyn. *Mervyn LeRoy: Take One* (New York: Hawthorne, 1974).

Lockwood, Charles. *Dream Palaces* (New York: Viking, 1981), pp. cover, 42, 43, 49, 56–62, 91.

Longstreet, Stephen. *All Star Cast* (New York: Crowell, 1977), ch. 24.

McCabe, John. *Charlie Chaplin* (Garden City: Doubleday, 1978), p. 76.

____, et al. *Laurel & Hardy* (New York: Dutton, 1975).

Monaco, James, *The Encyclopedia of Film* (New York: Perigee, 1991).

Morella, Joe, and Epstein, Edward. *The "It" Girl* (New York: Delacorte, 1976), pp. 5, 24, 30–31.

Morison, Samuel E. *The Oxford History of the American People* (New York: Oxford, 1965), p. 906.

Negri, Pola. *Memoirs of a Star* (Garden City, NY: Doubleday, 1970), p. 429.

Palmer, Edwin. *History of Hollywood* (Hollywood: Cawston, 1937), pp. 104–194.

Parish, James R. *The Fox Girls* (New Rochelle, NY: Arlington, 1971), pp. 16–38.

Parsons, Louella. *The Gay Illiterate* (Garden City, NY: Garden City, 1945), pp. 33–34.

Peary, Danny. *Close-Ups: The Movie Star Book* (New York: Workman, 1978), pp. 123–126.

Pickford, Mary. *Sunshine and Shadow* (Garden City, NY: Doubleday, 1955), pp. 314, 317.

Pisani, Ferri. *Au Pays du Film* (Paris: Librairie Plon, 1923), pp. 7–10.

Plays Produced in New York, (n.d.), p. 565. Cincinnati Historical Society's Theatre Collection.

Pratt, George. *Spellbound in Darkness* (Greenwich: New York Graphic Society, 1973), pp. 233–237, 430.

Ramsaye, Terry. *A Million and One Nights* (New York: Simon & Schuster, 1926; reprint 1964), pp. 702–704, 712, 759.

Rhode, Eric. *A History of the Cinema* (New York: Hill & Wang, 1976), pp. 71–72.

Robinson, David. *The History of World Cinema* (New York: Stein & Day, 1981), pp. 74–75, 122.

Ronay, Gabriel. *The Truth About Dracula* (New York: Stein & Day, 1972), p. 164.

Rosten, Leo C. *The Many Worlds of L*e*o R*o*s*t*e*n* (New York: Harper, 1964), p. 131.

Schickel, Richard. *Pictorial History of the Movies* (New York: Basic Books, 1964), p. 60.

____. *The Stars* (New York: Bonanza, 1962), pp. 30–31.

Schlesinger, Arthur. *The Rise of the City, 1878–1898* (New York: Macmillan, 1933), pp. 112, 271, 272, 305.

Schulberg, Bud. *Moving Pictures: Memories of a Hollywood Prince* (New York: Stein & Day, 1981), pp. 81–82, 176–177.

Shipman, David. *The Great Movie Stars: The Golden Years* (New York: Crown, 1970), pp. 39–41.

Silver, Alain, and Ursini, James. *The Vampire Film* (New York: Barnes, 1975), pp. 32, 40, 47.

Sinclair, Upton. *Upton Sinclair Presents William Fox* (Los Angeles: self published, 1933), pp. 12–13, 46, 56–57, 69, 185.

Smith, Gene. *When the Cheering Stopped* (New York: Morrow, 1967), p. 138.

Spehr, Paul. *The Movies Begin: Making Movies in New Jersey, 1887–1920* (Newark: Newark Museum, 1977), pp. 92–93, 118–119.

Starr, Kevin. *Inventing the Dream* (New York: Oxford, 1985), pp. 317–320.

Sullivan, Mark. *Our Times* (New York: Scribners, 1926–35), vol. 6 (The Twenties), p. 551.

Summers, Montague. *The Vampire in Europe* (New Hyde Park, New York: University Books, 1962), cited in Hamilton, *Theda Bara and the Vamp Phenomenon, 1915–1920*.

Thomas, Dana. *Lords of the Land* (New York: Putnam, 1971), pp. 241–245.

Thomson, David. *A Biographical Dictionary of Film* (New York: Morrow, 1981), p. 31.

Time-Life Books. *This Fabulous Century* (New York: Time-Life, 1970), vol. II, (1910-20), pp. 59, 263; vol. III, (1920–30), p. 45.

Torrence, Bruce. *Hollywood: The First 100 Years* (New York: Zoetrope, 1982), pp. 94, 98.

Underwood, Peter. *The Life of Boris Karloff* (New York: Drake, 1972), p. 78.

Wagenknecht, Edward, and Slide, Anthony. *The Films of D.W. Griffith* (New York: Crown, 1975), p. 182.

Wakeman, John. *World Film Directors* (New York: Wilson, 1987), vol. 1 (1890–1945).

Walker, Alexander. *The Celluloid Sacrifice: Aspects of Sex in the Movies* (New York: Hawthorne, 1966), pp. 19–27.

Weaver, John. *Los Angeles: The Enormous Village* (Santa Barbara: Capra, 1980), p. 83.

Webb, Michael, ed. *Hollywood: Legend and Reality* (Washington: Smithsonian and Boston: Little, Brown, 1986), pp. 117, 186.

Wenden, D. J. *The Birth of the Movies* (New York: Dutton, 1975), p. 112.

Wilk, Max. *The Wit and Wisdom of Hollywood* (New York: Atheneum, 1971), pp. 1, 16.

Wing, Ruth, ed. *The Blue Book of the Screen* (Hollywood: Blue Book, 1924), pp. 6–7.

Wolf, Leonard. *A Dream of Dracula* (Boston: Little, Brown, 1972), pp. 19, 114, 120, 122, 210, 213, 257.

ARTICLES

Most of the following articles are found in collections such as those of the Film Study Center and the Theatre Arts Library. Often their source is hand-noted. In the vast majority of cases these are correct; however, a check of *Newspapers in Microform* (1973), the Library of Congress' monumental listing of American newspapers, finds several of those publications not listed on the dates cited. Further, though there is no more complete listing of newspapers since the seventeenth century, the compilers of *Newspapers in Microform* do not claim 100 percent accuracy.

Signed Newspaper, Magazine and Journal Articles

Ashley, Leonard. "Flicks, Flacks and Flux," *Names*, December 1975, p. 232.

Bara, Theda. "How I Became a Film Vampire," *Forum*, June 1919, pp. 715-727, July 1919, pp. 83–93.

_____. "I'll Be a Tragedienne by Theda Bara," *Chicago Press*, April 14, 1916.

_____. "My Wild, Free, Untrammeled Carmen," *New York Evening Mail*, October 23, 1915.

_____. "Theda Bara's Defense," *Motion Picture*, August 1916, pp. 99–100.

Bell, Archie. "Psh! Theda Is Now Shedding Her Skin," *Cleveland* (OH) *Leader*, July 28, 1918.

_____. "Theda Bara — The Vampire Woman," *Theatre*, November 1915, p. 246.

_____. "Theda the Vampire," *Cleveland* (OH) *Leader*, October 24, 1915.

Blackstone, Lillian. "Sandwich à la Movie," *Photoplay*, February 1916.

Brady, Thomas F. "DeSylva Working on Movie of Bara," *New York Times*, January 21, 1949.

Brock, Alan. "The Unfulfilled Dream of a Star," *Classic Film Collector*, Fall 1969, pp. 6–8.

Brown, Alice C. "Cleopatra," *Ohio State Journal*, January 26, 1918.

Calistro, Paddy. "Taking Cues," *Los Angeles Times*, February 28, 1988, Magazine, p. 24.

Conlon, "Scoop." "Theda Bara to 'Come Back' in New Roles in Films," *San Francisco Chronicle*, March 12, 1922, p. 1D.

Coughlin, Gene. "Theda Bara, Famed 'Vamp,' Succumbs," *Los Angeles Herald-Examiner*, April 8, 1955, p. 1.

Courtlandt, Roberta. "The Divine Theda," *Motion Picture*, April 1917, pp. 59–62.

Dorn, Norman. "Theda Bara Was an Exotic Vamp from Cincinnati," *San Francisco Chronicle*, November 18, 1973, *Datebook* Magazine.

Doyle, Walter. "Theda Bara Finds Real Love Beside the Camera," *San Francisco Chronicle*, July 9, 1921.

Franklin, Wallace. "Purgatory's Ivory Angel," *Photoplay*, September 1915.

Grierson, John. "Putting Atmosphere in Pictures," *Motion Picture News*, December 4, 1926, pp. 2141–2142.

Hall, Gladys. "Salome," *Motion Pictures*, August 1918.

Johaneson, Bland. "Theda Bara, First Vamp, Back in Tryout Sketch," *Mirror*, November 20, 1929.

Kingsley, Grace. "How Stars Live Down Their Handicaps," *Los Angeles Times*, July 1, 1923, p. III–29.

_____. "Theda Bara Captures Thief," *Los Angeles Times*, November 4, 1926, p. II–8.

_____. "Theda Bara Returns," *Los Angeles Times*, May 3, 1923.

_____. "Theda Bara to Come Back in Vaudeville," *Los Angeles Times*, July 9, 1929, p. II–8.

_____. "Vamp Comes Back," *Los Angeles Times*, November 11, 1925, p. II–9.

Lawrence, Florence. "At Last — Theda Bara Has Been Seen in the Flesh," *Los Angeles Examiner*, February 21, 1919.

Lerman, Leo. "Living Legends," *Harpers Bazaar*, September 1948, p. 191.

Lipke, Katherine. "What Does Fate Plan for Bara?" *Los Angeles Times*, August 2, 1925, p. III–18.

Lockwood, Charles. "Priestess of Sin," *Horizon*, January 1981, pp. 64–69.

McKelvie, Martha G. "O-o-o-h! Theda," *Motion Picture World*, September 1918.

Mahoney, Vincent. "New 'Vamp' Sought for Scare Film," *New York Post*, October 20, 1934.

Maxwell, Virginia. "White Woman in the Jungle," *Photoplay*, September 1933, pp. 50–51, 109–111.

Mullet, Mary. "Theda Bara — Queen of the Vampires," *American Magazine*, September 1920, pp. 34-35.

Parsons, Louella. "How Greatest Film Vampire Makes Cleopatra Live Again," *Chicago Herald*, September 30, 1917.

_____. "Soul of Buddha," *Chicago Herald*, May 11, 1918.

Perelman, S. J. "Cloudland Revisited: The Wickedest Woman in Larchmont," *New Yorker*, October 18, 1952, pp. 34–36.

Ritchie, Marion B. "The Girl Who Made 'Theda' a Household Word," *Screenland*, February 1928.

Roberts, Arthur. "It's Hard Work for Theda to Play Vampire Roles," *Cleveland Plain Dealer*, September 18, 1915.

Roberts, George. "To Theda Bara," *Photoplay*, July 1918.

St. Johns, Adela. "The Hollywood Story," *American Weekly*, October 15, 1950, pp. 20–21.

Sanburn, Curt. "The Race to Save America's Film Heritage," *Life*, July 1985, pp. 69–80.

Sarett, Lew. "Ballade of a Rheumatic Vampire," *Motion Picture*, April 1918.

Scheuer, Philip. "Vamps Still Practice Art That Theda Bara Perfected," *Los Angeles Times*, April 17, 1955, p. IV-2

Seldes, Gilbert. "The Other Side of IT," *Century Magazine*, July 1929, pp. 297–302.

Smith, Fred J. "Keeping That Appointment with Theda Bara," *Motion Picture Classic*, February 1919.

Soanes, Wood. "Theda Bara Cinematic in 'Fata Morgana'," *Oakland Tribune*, June 8, 1931, p. B-19.

Stokes, Richard. "Cleopatra Movie Lavish Waste of Rich Resources," *St. Louis Post-Dispatch*, December 26, 1917.

Thomas, Bob. "What's in a Name? Plenty, in the Movies," *Fresno Bee*, July 19, 1986, p. D-6.

Tinée, Mae. "Tricks of Bara Wiggle Through Soul of Buddha," *Chicago Tribune*, cited in Hamilton, *Theda Bara and the Vamp Phenomenon, 1915–1920*, p. 52.

Vaught, Emily. "Muscular System of a Serpent," cited in Hamilton, *Theda Bara and the Vamp Phenomenon, 1915–1920*, p. 28.

Vincent-Baywood, Aileen. "The Arab Immigrants," *Aramco World Magazine*, Sept.-Oct. 1986, pp. 11–15.

Von Blon, Katherine. "Theda Bara Scores in 'Bella Donna' Drama," *Los Angeles Times*, May 24, 1934, p. I-12.

Walker, Betty. "Theda Bara Writes Book," *San Francisco Examiner*, November 17, 1925.

Wallace, Carol, ed. "100 Years of Hollywood," *People Weekly*, February 9, 1987, pp. 25–84.

Weitzel, Edward. "Her Greatest Love," *Motion Picture World*, April 21, 1917.

Whitaker, Alma. "Stars' Names Banned from Exclusive Lists," *Los Angeles Times*, December 2, 1934, p. II-1.

Williams, Joe. "Being a Letter of Explanation to One Theda Bara Vampire," *Cleveland Leader*, January 6, 1918.

Woollcott, Alexander. "The Play: The Blue Flame," review, *New York Times*, March 16, 1920, p. 18.

____. "The Success of the Season" (review of *The Blue Flame*), *Century*, July 1920, p. 413.

Young, Marguerite. "You Remember Theda Bara, Vampire of the Screen? Well, Her Blonde Sister Writes Jungle Movie Thrillers," *New York World-Telegram*, June 26, 1933.

Unsigned Newspaper, Magazine and Journal Articles

"The Art of Impersonation Is Shrewdly Cultivated on Our Current Stage," *Stage*, January 1934, p. 32.

"Boston Theatre," *Boston Post*, March19, 1918.

"A Century of Cleopatras," *Theatre Arts*, December 1947, pp. 23–26.

"Changing Modes in Vampires," *Vanity Fair*, January 1932, pp. 34–35.

"City Short of Quota by Over Four Million," *Los Angeles Times*, April 26, 1918, p. II-2.

"Cleopatra Big Hit at the Casino," *Spokesman Review* (Spokane, WA), January 20, 1918.

"Come Home—All Is Forgiven," *Photoplay*, February 1923, p. 44.

"Evil to Him Who Evil Thinks, Says Theda," *Toledo Blade*, February 13, 1919.

"Exceptional Photoplay: FLESH AND THE DEVIL," *National Board of Review Magazine*, February 1927, pp. 11–13.

"Final Curtain for Theda Bara," *Cincinnati Enquirer*, April 8, 1955.

"A Fool There Was," *Variety*, May 12, 1915.

"The Forbidden Path," *Columbus Journal*, April 27, 1918.

"44th Street Theatre," *Theatre*, November 1918.

"Friday Liberty Day," *Los Angeles Times*, April 24, 1918, p. II-2.

"A Gay History of Hollywood," *Photoplay*, October 1948, p. 34.

"Girls, Watch Your Step!" *Los Angeles Times*, April 23, 1923, p. II-5.

"Her Luxuriant Hair Qualification for Job," *Louisville Post*, November 1, 1915.

"I Wonder What's Become of … Theda Bara," *Los Angeles Mirror*, September 9, 1934, *Sunday* Magazine, p. 13.

"In the Wake of the News," *New York Post*, September 26, 1933.

"Just Finished Stock Tour," *New York Morning Telegraph*, July 2, 1931.

"Kathleen Mavourneen," *Variety*, August 22, 1919.

"Lady from Cincinnati" (editorial), *New York Times*, April 9, 1955, p. 12.

"Living Legends," *Harpers Bazaar*, September 1948, p. 191.

"London as a Vampire," *New York Times*, March 28, 1920, p. VI-2.

"Meet Them Again," *Stage*, January 1934.

"New Fairbanks 'Thriller'," *New York Times*, September 11, 1916, p. 11.

"Of the Vampires of the Screen There's None So Bare as Theda," *Cleveland Plain Dealer*, September 13, 1918.

"Poor Theda Bara Loses Another Waste," *New York Mail*, January 24, 1916.

"Revamping the Vampire," *Nation*, August 10, 1921, p. 140.

"Rumor Has Theda Bara Returning to Screen," *San Francisco Chronicle*, May 17, 1925.

"Salome," *Variety*, October 1918.

"The Screen," *New York Times*, August 20, 1919, p. 12.

"Screen Favorites and a Stage Debutante," *Theatre*, December 1921, p. 384.

"Services Being Arranged for Silent Screen's Siren," *Cincinnati Enquirer*, April 9, 1955.

"Shakespeare Movie Way," *New York Times*, October 23, 1916, p. 10.

"Silent Film Era 'Vamp' Theda Bara Succumbs," *Los Angeles Times*, April 8, 1955, p. 1.

"Sister Gets Bulk of $100,000 Estate from Theda Bara," *Cincinnati Enquirer*, April 19, 1955.

"Sister to Get Most of Theda Bara's $100,000," *Los Angeles Times*, April 19, 1955, p. I-21.

"Some 500,000 Spectators Follow Her Every Day," *New York Times*, February 20, 1916, p. II-8.

"Southern California Goes Over the Top on Liberty Day," *Los Angeles Times*, April 27, 1918, p. II-1.

"Talk of the Town: Theda Bara Mystery Solved," *Cincinnati Enquirer*, April 11, 1955.

"Tank Drive in Streets to Sell Liberty Bonds," *Los Angeles Times*, April 20, 1918, p. 1.

"Theda Bara" (editorial), *Cincinnati Enquirer*, April 11, 1955.

"Theda Bara," *Life*, December 22, 1958.

"Theda Bara as Cleopatra," *New York Times*, October 15, 1917, p. 11.

"Theda Bara as Egypt," *Springfield Union*, November 23, 1917.

"Theda Bara Breaks All Bond-Selling Records," *Los Angeles Times*, April 27, 1918, p. II-3.

"Theda Bara Calls Garbo Greatest All-Time 'Vamp'," *New York World-Telegram*, April 20, 1934.

"Theda Bara Dies, Screen Star, 65," *New York Times*, April 8, 1955, p. 21.

"Theda Bara Entertains," *New York Mirror*, February 8, 1939.

"Theda Bara, Film Star, Suffering from Prostration," *San Francisco Chronicle*, September 25, 1918.

"Theda Bara Films Orient in 'Salome'," *New York Times*, October 7, 1917, p. 11.

"Theda Bara Films Test Plot Writers," *New York Times*, January 24, 1916, p. 12.

"Theda Bara Gets Carloads of Xmas Gifts," *New York Telegraph*, January 6, 1918.

"Theda Bara Has Play That Fits Her," *Chicago Daily News*, October 13, 1915.

"Theda Bara in Real Thrill," *New York Times*, September 5, 1921, p. 12.

"Theda Bara in 'The Red Devil'," *New York Telegraph*, November 18, 1929.

"Theda Bara Is Doing Real Acting Now," *Cleveland Plain Dealer*, March 21, 1916.

"Theda Bara Legend Lives On," *New York Journal American*, October 8, 1939.

"Theda Bara News, Maybe Last Time! Gems to Be Sold," *Cincinnati Enquirer*, April 29, 1957.

"Theda Bara Pleads for Glamour," *Screen Weekly*, August 6, 1932, p. 9.

"Theda Bara Resumes Career," *Los Angeles Times*, May 10, 1934.

"Theda Bara Returns from Abroad," *New York Times*, August 19, 1920, p. 9.

"Theda Bara Returns to Screen," *Los Angeles Times*, March 14, 1926, p. III-27.

"Theda Bara, Silent Film 'Vamp,' Dies," *San Francisco Chronicle*, April 8, 1955, p. 9.

"Theda Bara Surprises," *Los Angeles Times*, January 20, 1929, p. 1.

"Theda Bara Tells How She Wrote 'Soul of Buddha'," *Los Angeles Examiner*, May 12, 1918.

"Theda Bara to Appear in Carmen; Movies' Biggest Battle Near," *Cleveland Leader*, September 18, 1915.

"Theda Bara to Be Here for Jubilee," *San Francisco Chronicle*, September 3, 1925.

"Theda Bara Up to Old Tricks in Revised Sapho," *Columbus Citizen*, May 22, 1916.

"Theda Bara Voted 'The Ideal Carmen' by Immense Crowds at the Mary Austin," *Louisville Post*, November 1, 1915.

"Theda Bara Wins Irish Shawl," *Cleveland News*, September 21, 1919.

"Theda Bara's Comeback," *Variety*, April 16, 1934.

"Theda Bara's Will Is Filed," *New York Times*, April 19, 1955, p. 21.

"Theda in Vaudeville," *Exhibit Review*, September 10, 1929.

"Theda Is Through Vamping," *Los Angeles Times*, November 17, 1925, p. II-11.

"Theda Makes 'Em All Baras," *New York Times*, November 17, 1917, p. 11.

"Theda Quits Vampire Roles," *Boston Post*, November 16, 1925.

"Theda Staging a Comeback," *Film Daily*, January 2, 1923.

"'To Bara' Means to Vamp; She's at the Orpheum Now," *Cleveland Leader*, August 4, 1918.

"Two New Feature Films," *New York Times*, March 13, 1916, p. 5.

"A Vamp Worshipper," *Cleveland Leader*, January 28, 1918.

"Vamping in Movies Suffices: This Star Prefers Normality in Real Life," *Cleveland Plain Dealer*, February 20, 1916.

"The Vampire of the Screen," *Green Book*, February 1916, pp. 263–265.

"Veterans of Film World Honored," *Los Angeles Times*, November 10, 1953.

"Wickedest Face in the World More Wicked Than Ever," *Montgomery* (AL) *Journal*, May 13, 1915.

"Women Must Choose to Love or Be Loved — Says Vampire," *Peoria Journal*, May 6, 1916.

Newspapers and Magazines Cited Without Article Titles

Brooklyn Daily Eagle, December 18, 1917.

California Historical Courier, April-May 1986, p. 5.

Cleveland Plain Dealer, March 9, 1916, March 11, 1916, January 11, 1918.

Cleveland Press, January 19, 1918.

Detroit News Tribune, July 30, 1915.

Dramatic Mirror (New York), January 20, 1915, April 21, 1915.

Film Daily, September 11, 1931.

Hollywood Reporter, October 16, 1932.

Literary Digest, May 16, 1936, p. 23.

London Times, April 21, 1955.

Los Angeles Examiner, February 28, 1916.

Los Angeles Times, October 16, 1925.

Louisville (KY) *Herald*, April 13, 1915, October 29, 1915.

Marysville [CA] *Appeal*, November 14, 1915, p. 6.

New York Journal American, February 14, 1939.

New York Telegraph, November 3, 1915, December 17, 1915, December 27, 1915, December 15, 1923.

New York Times, November 1, 1915, p. 11; May 8, 1916, p. 9; October 7, 1918, June 21, 1921; October 20, 1923; November 12, 1925; June 4, 1926, November 23, 1927; June 30, 1954; July 1, 1954; August 11, 1954; March 23, 1955; March 27, 1955; March 28, 1955; July 8, 1957; November 6, 1957.

Oakland [CA] *Tribune*, April 8, 1955.

Philadelphia Press, January 25, 1916.

Philadelphia Public Ledger, June 8, 1919.

Photoplay, October 1921, p. 52; May 1924; July 1926; August 1929; February 1931, p. 134; September 1931, p. 38; March 1932, p. 39; November 1935, p. 51; August 1939, p. 32; October 1939, p. 43; October 1948.

Picture Show, May 3, 1919, October 2, 1920.

Springfield [MA] *Union*, November 21, 1915.

Syracuse [New York] *Post Standard*, April 20, 1915.

Theatre, December 1921, p. 384.

Time, December 26, 1949, p. 24; April 18, 1955, p. 104.

Variety, December 3, 1915, June 21, 1918, December 6, 1918, January 25, 1919, June 13, 1919, April 13, 1955.

Unidentified Articles from New York's Film Study Center

"A Line or Two," January 6, 1920.

"Attorney Fells Rumor That Fair Theda's Broke," December 19, 1923.

"Bara Out of Fox," August 2, 1919.

"Bara to Release Through Burr," October 5, 1923.

"Brabin-Bara Rift Surprising," December 15, 1923.

"Court Legalizes Film Star's Name," no source.

"'Easiest Way' Is for Theda Bara," November 19, 1922.

"'The Easiest Way,' Stage Play Chosen by Selznick for Theda Bara's Picture," December 2, 1922.

"Ex-Film Siren Is Commentator on International Life, Events and Bathtubs," 1939.

"Famous Film Star Gets Rights to Name Theda Bara," no source.

"$15,000 for Drawing Contract," December 14, 1919.

"Film's Famous Vamp Marrying, Broadway Hears," May 10, 1921.

"In the Courts," January 26, 1920.

"More Bara-Fox Trouble," June 13, 1919.

"Movie Relief Fund Given $200,000," *Los Angeles Times*, January 1966.

"New Theda Bara Sketch," November 23, 1929.

"Ochs to Star Theda Bara," June 7, 1922.

"Producers After Theda Bara," January 1919.

"Selznick Denies That Story for Theda Bara Has Been Selected," June 22, 1922.

"Spoiling a Perfectly Good Yarn," February 1920.

"Started It," no date.

"Suing Theda," December 1919.

"The Brabins Return," August 15, 1921.

"Theda Bara," 1920 (opening sentence: "She's Mrs. Tom Bodkin Now...." 1920.

"Theda Bara a Blonde," December 13, 1917.

'Theda Bara Buys New Certificate," July 22, 1919.

"Theda Bara Completes 27th Picture," December 1917.

"Theda Bara Film Causes Riots," February 10, 1920.

"Theda Bara Has Done 32 Films for William Fox Company," July 1918.

"Theda Bara Here to Work," October 28, 1923.

"Theda Bara Ill," n. d.

"Theda Bara Is Going West to Join Husband," May 27, 1923.

"Theda Bara Is Here," August 22, 1923.

"Theda Bara Leases the Randolph Miner Place," 1918.

"Theda Bara in 'The Unchastened Woman'," September 21, 1925.

"Theda Bara in Tour of Personal Appearances," August 27, 1921.

"Theda Bara Is Made Actress' Legal Name," November 17, 1917.

"Theda Bara Is 'On the Fence'," December 11, 1924.

"Theda Bara, Maybe," October 13, 1923.

'Theda Bara Productions Has Been Formed," May 13, 1924.

'Theda Bara Returning," February 19, 1922.

"Theda Bara, the Film Star, Wedded Secretly to C.J. Brabin," July 8, 1921.

"Theda Bara to Appear in Her Own Play," 1918.

'Theda Bara to Be Here," 1918.

"Theda Bara to Return to Films," November 11, 1925.

"Theda Bara to Show Them 'It' As It Is," July 11, 1931.

"Theda Bara's Brother Has Joined the Army," 1918.

"Theda Bara's Personal Tour," August 1, 1921.

"Theda Bara's Stage Salary Exceeds Her Picture Income," April 2, 1920.

"Theda Bara's Tour," September 1, 1921.

"Theda Coming Back," August 10, 1921.

"Theda Returning," July 17, 1928.

"Vamps — Bara to...," February 23, 1936.

"Was in Hurry to Drive Theda Bara," June 1918.

"What About Theda?" no date.

"Will Theda Bara Play in Goldwyn's 'Three Weeks'?" June 25, 1923.

No headline, opening sentence "A recent query here as to the whereabouts of Theda Bara...." February 25, 1933.

No headline, opening sentence "Confirming our story ... Theda Bara was flirting with a movie contract under the Chadwick...." *New York Mirror*, December 12, 1924.

No headline, opening sentence "Myron Selznick ... announces ...that he has completed arrangements...." July 8, 1922.

No headline, opening sentence "Theda Bara ... goes to Italy...." No date.

No headline, opening sentence: "Theda Bara has joined her husband...." May 21, 1923.

No headline, opening sentence "Theda Bara, having quit the screen... is about to try matrimony." April 2, 1921.

No headline, opening sentence "Theda Bara is leaving this week...." September 7, 1929.

No headline, opening sentence "Theda Bara, thoroughly rested...." October 2, 1918.

No headline, opening sentence "Two pictures of Theda Bara — one as Cincinnatians saw her...." November 1915.

LISTINGS IN DIRECTORIES, YEARBOOKS, ETC.

Americana Annual: 1956, p. 75.
Cumulative Book Index, January 1928.
United States Catalogue, July 1925–December 1927.
Walnut Hills High School, Cincinnati, 1903 Yearbook.
Who Was Who in America (Chicago: Marquis, 1963), vols. I–III.

INTERVIEWS AND LETTERS

Bann, Richard. Los Angeles. Telephone conversations, December 5, 1987, April 2, 1994.

Barberich, Kathy. Fresno, California. Conversation, August 25, 1987.

Belzberg, Hyman. Beverly Hills. Conversation, February 6, 1988.

Beverly Hills Women's Club. Telephone conversation, July 2, 1987.

Cincinnati Historical Society. Telephone conversation, July 1, 1986.

Coleman, Bob. Los Angeles. Interview, August 29, 1990.

Columbia Studio, Public Relations Department. Telephone conversation, June 20, 1988.

Davies, Wallace. Letter to Cincinnati Public Library, February 15, 1968, Cincinnati Historical Society.

_____. Letters to John Mullane, February 27 and March 10, 1968, Cincinnati Historical Society.

Furstman, Edward. West Los Angeles. Interview, August 29, 1990.

Gumfudgin, Ormsby. La Crescenta, California. Letter, February 11, 1991.

Hicks, Jay. Chula Vista, California. Letter, August 17, 1990.

Kisro, Diane. Venice, California. Interview, August 29, 1990.

Leach, Virginia. Piedmont, California. Letter, September 10, 1987.

Liebman, Roy, letter to Mr. Bork, September 11, 1967, Cincinnati Historical Society.

McClintock, Virginia. West Covina, California. Letter, August 18, 1990.

Mullane, John. Letters to Wallace Davies, February 22, and March 1, 1968, Cincinnati Historical Society.

Panaggio, Leonard (*Newport* [RI] *Daily News*). Letter, June 23, 1986.

Pierce Brothers Mortuary. Glendale, California. Telephone conversation, June 20, 1986.

Plank, Bryan. LaJolla, California. Letter, August 1990.

Rothlass, Eileen (Cincinnati Public Schools). Letter, June 20, 1986.

Schiefelin, Mrs. E., Los Angeles. Letter, August 21, 1990.

Shepherd, David (principal of Walnut Hills High School,Cincinnati). Letter, June 25, 1986.

Stanley, June Millarde. Gaithersburg, MD. Telephone conversation, February 13, 1987.

University of Cincinnati, Archives and Records Office. Telephone conversation, July 2, 1987.

THESES, DOCUMENTS, FILMS, AND COLLECTIONS

DeCordova, Richard. *The Emergence of the Star System in America: An Examination of the Institutional and Ideological Function of the Star: 1907–1922*. Ph.D. dissertation, University of California, Los Angeles, 1986.

A Fool There Was. 16mm film, Metropolitan Museum of Art, New York.

Goodman, Estie (Lori Bara). Birth certificate, Cincinnati Historical Society.

Hamilton, Gayla Jamison. *Theda Bara and the Vamp Phenomenon, 1915–1920.* M.A. thesis, University of Georgia, 1972.

Robinson Locke, Collection, New York Public Library Theatre Collection, Lincoln Center. Includes unsigned items.

Theda Bara File, Museum of Modern Art, New York, Film Study Center. Includes items unsigned, undated or unattributed.

United States Twelfth Census (1900). Vol. 70, E.D. 272, Sheet 4, Line 17 (Soundex Ohio G355).

Index